better than PERFECT

**7 STRATEGIES
TO CRUSH YOUR INNER CRITIC**
and CREATE A LIFE YOU LOVE

better than

PERFECT

DR. ELIZABETH LOMBARDO

SEAL PRESS

Author's Note: The names of all clients and most of the others who appear in the stories and anecdotes have been changed to protect their privacy. I have also created composites of most people, so they are not identifiable.

SEAL PRESS
A Member of the Perseus Books Group
1700 Fourth Street
Berkeley, California 94710

Library of Congress Cataloging-in-Publication Data
Lombardo, Elizabeth.
Better than perfect : 7 strategies to crush your inner critic and create a life you love / Elizabeth Lombardo.
ISBN 978-1-58005-549-9 (paperback)
1. Perfectionism (Personality trait) 2. Imperfection. 3. Self-acceptance. 4. Happiness. I. Title.
BF698.35.P47L66 2014
155.2'32--dc23
2014020639

10 9 8 7 6 5 4 3 2 1

Cover design by Faceout Studio, Kara Davison
Interior design by Megan Jones Design

Printed in the United States of America
Distributed by Publishers Group West

To Jeffrey, for your unconditional love and support.
Thank you for helping me see how amazing
Better Than Perfect can be.

And to all the people out there who are tired of not
feeling good enough. You *are* Better Than Perfect.

Contents

Introduction

I'VE BEEN A perfectionist for most of my life.

In all honesty, I've been rewarded quite nicely because of it.

At the same time, though, it's caused a lot of unnecessary tears, tension, and trials for me and for the people around me.

It was 7:27 in the morning. I'd already been up a few hours trying to tackle my lengthy to-do list before flying to New York around noon. I still had to pack, wondering what shoes I should bring; respond to a journalist about how to excel during change in the workplace; empty the dishwasher; get my daughters' breakfasts ready; and test my eight-year-old on her spelling words.

My stress level was definitely up there, but I was trying to keep it together.

"Unpleasant," I said, reciting a word from the spelling list.

As I glanced over my daughter's shoulder, she wrote the word down on a sheet of paper. UNPLEASANT. Two E's rather than two A's. Hmmm.

*When she misspelled unpleasant, I started to get unpleas-
ant. Part of it was that I'd always had trouble with spelling.
(I love spell-check!) But the bigger problem was that I was
a perfectionist, and my being a perfectionist at that moment
could have made both my daughter and me very unhappy.*

*"Your test is today, Sweetheart," I said in what I hoped
was a motivating tone. In reality, I was really anxious, thinking she'd miss that word on the test.*

*Now, as I sit here recounting this incident, I'm embar-
rassed that my daughter's messing up one letter would upset
me so much. Unfortunately, it did.*

*I've always tried to hide my perfectionist tendencies from
my children, hoping to not pass them on to my girls. But who
was I kidding here? The tension in our kitchen was palpable.*

*Then my daughter saved the day. "Mom, I think we all
need to take a deep breath," she said.*

*This was the proverbial wisdom out of the mouth of a
child. But for me it was much more than that: it was an important wake-up call.*

On some level, perfectionism is rewarded in our society. We may
be the person who consistently stays at work until midnight—to complete a project in particular, or to excel at our job in general. Maybe
we're striving to have the body of a supermodel or a superhero. Or we
might go above and beyond "normal" expectations to ensure our children get into Harvard. As you might guess, many champion athletes,
prominent scientists, and celebrities demonstrate perfectionist traits.
Serena Williams, a number-one-ranked female tennis player and the

only female player to win over $50 million in prize money, describes herself this way: "I'm a perfectionist. I'm pretty much insatiable."

Of course, not *all* of us are extreme perfectionists like Serena Williams. And yet, many of us have one or more perfectionistic thought patterns or behaviors that negatively impact our lives on a daily basis—from our relationships to our work.

Do any of these tendencies sound familiar?

- You see your life in black-and-white terms. "I did not get the promotion; I am a failure." Or, "I ate one cookie and ruined my diet; might as well eat the entire bag."

- You often act out of fear rather than passion. Fear would say: "This project is so stressful. I could get fired if I mess it up." Whereas passion would say: "I enjoy using my strengths and collaborating with others to make this project incredible."

- You've made up tons of rules for yourself (and others) that you don't even know you're following. "I should be more success-ful." "I should be in better shape." "She should call me more." "He should do the dishes since I cooked dinner."

- You give up before you've even tried to do something, like compete for a promotion or take on a challenging assignment. You think, "I failed in the past, so why risk trying again?" Or, "If it's never really going to happen, then why bother?"

- You frequently use distorted thinking when you make deci-sions. You think you can read the minds of those around you. "She thinks I'm lazy." "He doesn't love me." Or you predict the future will be unbearable, essentially making a

mountain out of a molehill. "My career will be ruined if I
mess up this speech!"

Sounds pretty unpleasant, however you spell it! But there's
more . . .

- Chances are you experience high levels of stress, rarely feel
  satisfied, and live with a barrage of negative self-talk cycling
  around your head. You consistently think, "If only I achieve
  X, then I'll be happy." Happiness is seen as the endgame, the
  result of achieving a goal. Your self-confidence is conditional,
  based on how "successful" you view yourself at that moment,
  or on how others react to you.

- Maybe your health is not where you want it to be. You may
  be overweight, struggling to stay on a weight-loss program, or
  underweight and starving yourself—or even average weight but
  obsessing about food. Or, you experience insomnia from all
  the endless chatter in your head, its volume increasing the moment your head hits the pillow. Or you experience medically
  unexplained aches or pains that drain your energy and enjoyment of life.

- Your relationships may not be as happy or fulfilling as you'd
  like them to be. You may prioritize other people and tasks
  above your own fun, your own needs for relaxing or recharg-
  ing—sometimes even above the needs of your family. And don't
  kid yourself. They notice and resent it.

- When it comes to work, you put in excessive hours and are rarely fully satisfied with your results. Alternatively, there may be times when you procrastinate starting or finishing a project, for fear you won't be able to complete the task perfectly. You may have difficulty making decisions, repeatedly second-guessing yourself. You feel there is "never enough time," or that you are doomed to fall short of someone's expectations—or your own.

Do any of these unhappy descriptions sound like you? I thought so. That's why I wrote *Better Than Perfect*. Because you're likely tired— no, exhausted—by the incessant drive to control the future, and by the unsatisfying feeling that, no matter how hard you try, you will always come up short—always less than you could or should be. I know these feelings, because I've been there.

"I'm a perfectionist. I can't help it, I get really upset with myself if I fail in the least."
—JUSTIN TIMBERLAKE

SO, WHAT'S THE PROBLEM?

From their standpoint, perfectionists often don't see anything wrong with how they are, and they frequently rationalize their standards, thinking, "Of course I want to strive for the best! Why would I settle for being mediocre?"

In fact, many are petrified by the idea of giving up their perfectionism, as it's become their way of living and (sometimes) succeeding.

And they may even see forgoing these perfectionist patterns as failure. I understand that fear of letting go—it's something I've struggled with myself.

But, while the goal of perfectionism is to feel good about yourself, it actually has the opposite effect. Why? Because there's always that awful inner critic constantly judging you, saying, "You're just not good enough." (Or worse.)

In my private practice, I work with a lot of perfectionists. Most of them don't come in saying, "I need help with my perfectionism." Usually they seek my help to deal with the often dire *consequences* of their perfectionism: depression, stress, insomnia, strained relationships, health problems, work concerns.

"Perfectionism becomes a badge of honor with you playing the part of the suffering hero."
—DAVID D. BURNS, PSYCHIATRIST

My purpose here is not to pathologize what you are doing or tell you that you need to change. I am not asking you to give up who you are or become someone you are not. I promise not to give you clichéd advice such as:

- "Stop being so hard on yourself."

- "Those details are not important."

- "It doesn't have to be perfect."

- "Just stop worrying about it."

While these suggestions may make rational sense, most perfectionists don't actually believe in them. We also don't know how to apply them, or don't really want to. I know I didn't!

LIVE A BETTER THAN PERFECT LIFE

Let me ask you a few questions:

- What would your life be like if you had more contentment and less stress?

- What would it mean if you accomplished more with less time and energy?

- How would it feel if you had peace of mind rather than all that self-imposed anxiety and pressure?

- How would being happier change how you interact with your family, friends, coworkers, and others?

Consider me your happiness coach. In the world we live in, being happy can be hard work. And I'm here to help you. I want you to be *truly* happy. Not just "looks good on paper so she should be happy." No, I want you to feel true joy and peace in your heart. I want you to start living a life of purpose and passion.

To that end I've created the Better Than Perfect program. The goal here is not necessarily "less perfectionism," but rather a more balanced and comprehensive sense of satisfaction and success. It will put *you* in control—not your perfectionism.

Whether you have a few perfectionist tendencies or are an extreme perfectionist, you can benefit from implementing the Better Than

Perfect program. It's time to crush the critic inside your head that keeps holding you back. These guidelines will help you live a happier, healthier, more successful and fulfilled life. They have worked miracles—large and small—in my life and in the lives of hundreds of my clients. They can work for you, too.

The result? A life you love.

Let me show you. Before applying the Better Than Perfect strategies, my concept of being "satisfied" meant settling—settling for a life that was less than perfect. Now I realize that satisfaction is an incredible state of feeling contented and gratified with the gifts—the people and experiences—that life offers me.

Thanks to having implemented this program, I've found my stress level is dramatically lower and my happiness level is much higher. Basically, I worry less and I laugh more.

I am more relaxed and better able to enjoy my children, husband, and friends. I no longer feel pressured to work all the time (yes, that used to be me incessantly checking my cell phone); I also no longer worry about what still needs to be done. My relationship with my husband has become much closer, and my daughters have told me I'm much more fun to be around. (Sure, that sentiment may change when they become teenagers, so I'll savor it for as long as I can!) The added benefit is that I am modeling the way I *want* my children to act and be—rather than the stressed out, nothing-is-good-enough parent I was before.

My sleep is much more restorative. I wake up in the morning excited about my day, ready to take on whatever comes.

Following the Better Than Perfect guidelines has also helped me be more successful. By "success" I mean something far more than my old definition of achieving certain milestones. I'm talking about feeling grateful for what is happening in my life, prioritizing my relationships, health, and happiness in addition to striving to excel at work—whereas previously excelling at work was my top priority. In my work life I used to operate out of fear; today I'm far more focused on passionately building my business. That's a really big change for me, and the results have been explosive.

To the surprise of my "old" self, living a Better Than Perfect life has also allowed me to fulfill greater achievement. For example, I used to be horribly anxious and fearful about speaking in public—terrified of messing up. Now it's not uncommon for me to speak in front of several million people, say on *The Today Show*, without stressing that I might screw up. Huge, right?

Throughout this book I'll be sharing the ways in which my perfectionism caused both benefits and blunders in my relationships, my business, my health, and throughout my life. You will also hear from a variety of others talking about their experiences. While the specifics you'll encounter may look different from what's going on in your life, I think you will see many similarities, too.

YOU'LL BE AMAZED AT THE DIFFERENCE!

Here's what you can expect to gain from applying the strategies of a Better Than Perfect life:

✓ Less worry

✓ Less stress

✓ More happiness

✓ Greater confidence, independent of results

✓ A healthier body

✓ Better sleep

✓ Happier, more fulfilling relationships

✓ Greater productivity with less effort

✓ Greater prosperity

✓ A life fueled by passion instead of by fear

✓ A strong sense of contentment

✓ More control over your life

You can expect to feel more successful in almost every corner of your life. Believe me, this is not just an empty promise. It's a pattern that I have helped create, both in my life and in my many clients' lives.

The truth is, you don't need your perfectionistic patterns in order for you to experience the success you've already enjoyed. You can achieve success *and* enjoy life, too! But that doesn't mean you need to change everything. Some parts of perfectionism that may be working for you likely include:

✓ Your passion to make positive change

✓ Your desire to truly feel good about yourself

✓ Your determination to make a difference

✓ Your commitment to having a positive influence on others

✓ Your inspiration to improve your life, the lives of others, and even the world

At the same time as you embrace your effective traits, are you equally ready to let go of the stuff that isn't working well, such as beating yourself up, working endless hours, procrastinating, and being driven by an overwhelming fear of failure?

If so, this book is for you. I want you to make this book *yours*. Argue with the things that don't work for you. Flag the parts you want to read again. Note your thoughts and observations. Start the process of transforming your life by answering the questions you'll find in every chapter. I invite you to thoroughly engage with this book. Getting your thoughts out of your head and onto paper will give you more insight into how perfectionist patterns may be affecting your life—and how you can make changes that work for you.

If you're ready to start making positive changes in your life, I'm here to help you. Let's get started!

PART ONE

Do You Strive to Be Perfect?

CHAPTER 1

What Is Perfectionism?

W HEN I TELL people I'm writing a book about perfectionism, I usually get one of three responses:

- ◆ "I *need* that!"

- ◆ "My wife/boss/sister/father *needs* that!"

- ◆ "I'm not a perfectionist."

The first group, which is predictably small, is self-selected and honest. The second group is much larger—everyone seems to know someone *else* who suffers from perfectionism. But the third group is by far the largest. Few of us, it seems, want to see ourselves as perfectionists. But all this changes when I explain what I mean when I talk about perfectionism. At that point, people in the last group inevitably say, "Wait, that's me!"

No matter what your first reaction is, you can still benefit from reading this book. Because even if you don't view yourself as a perfectionist, you may have some behaviors or tendencies associated with perfectionism. And it's likely that these traits have proved to be counterproductive or even damaging to your quality of life—your well-being, your sense of self, and the relationships you value most.

As a recovering perfectionist, I'm here to tell you that "perfectionism" doesn't mean perfect. Far from it. *Perfectionism* is defined as "a tendency to set standards that are unreasonably high and to measure an individual's worth in terms of ability to meet these standards." In reality, perfectionism is deeper than that, at least the way I define *perfectionism*. Let's look a little more closely at the features that perfectionists often exhibit. See if you can see yourself in any or all of these characteristics.

Perfectionists have extremely **high standards** that are nearly impossible to achieve on a consistent basis, and they experience serious distress when those standards aren't met. This extreme mind-set often carries over into unrealistic expectations of others.

Perfectionists view many aspects of life in **all-or-nothing** terms, such as "If I don't get 100 percent correct on the test I'm a failure." Perfectionists often view their own performance—as well as other people and experiences—as being one extreme or the other, either "all good" or "all bad." Unfortunately, this all-or-nothing worldview leaves little room for a sense of success, and lots of room for perceived failure.

One of the bigger ironies of this mind-set is that, despite the name, perfectionists don't think they're perfect at all. In fact, because "perfection" is the only acceptable level of success—and the reality is that no one is "perfect"—deep down, perfectionists tend to view themselves as **failures**. And so they focus on how not to feel like a failure.

At the core of perfectionism is a sense of **conditional self-worth**. Perfectionists equate their value with the achievement of specific, often unattainable goals. In their minds, they are only as good as their last accomplishment.

Perfectionists **beat themselves up** in their endless drive to be better. If you could stick a microphone inside their brains you'd hear their inner critics saying things like "I should have tried harder" or "I am such a loser." Perfectionists criticize themselves this way because they feel the need to be *better*—more successful, more prosperous, more "perfect." Ironically, though, this negative self-talk often has the opposite effect. It causes more stress and brings about less success.

Perfectionists also tend to be **reliant on other people's praise**, often basing their worth on how others react to them. Deep down, perfectionists often long to hear how impressed others are with the perfectionist's accomplishments, even if it makes them uncomfortable to receive that praise or they openly minimize what they've done. This desire for praise can be so strong that a perfectionist might put aside her own needs in order to garner that coveted praise. For instance, a woman may stay up all night working on a project for her boss, or skip her favorite "girls' night out" because the PTA requested her help on the same evening.

That perfectionists base their view of success on the praise of others is linked to another perfectionist trait: focus on, and fear of, **negative evaluation**. This trait robs perfectionists of the ability to achieve true happiness and a sense of peace. On the outside they may appear happy, but underneath that "perfect" shell is a barrage of frustration and anxiety that leads them to replay negative past events over and over (and over) for what they didn't do or shouldn't have done.

Perfectionists are more *motivated by fear* than they are motivated by the prospect of fun, especially fear of failure *and* being seen negatively by others. Their focus tends to be on how not to fail. The result is an internal concentration on self-judgments, like "What am I doing wrong?" and "What *should* I be doing?" rather than "What am I doing right?" and "What do I *want* to be doing?"

Though this may sound circular, perfectionists often have a *need for perfectionism*. As such, they are fearful of giving it up. They want to excel, to create excellence, to be the best. And they think their perfectionism is the only way to achieve this. It's true that some behaviors— the hard work, determination, perseverance, relentlessness, diligence, and striving—*can* assist with this. At the same time, the excessive worry, stress, unrealistic standards, and constant pressure can actually make us less efficient and successful in the long run. In effect, perfectionism can be *self-defeating*.

Perfectionists' fear of failure feeds *indecisiveness*. You can see this when perfectionists have a tough time making a decision: they're scared they'll choose "incorrectly." Their all-or-nothing thinking instills the belief that there is one answer that is "right," while the rest are "wrong." Perfectionists don't want to say the wrong thing—which they view as indication they themselves are wrong, bad, or not good enough—and as a result often avoid saying anything definitive at all. They also fear others will view their decisions as poor or stupid.

There is a great paradox behind all this: while many perfectionists are overachievers, sometimes they show up at the other end of the spectrum as *underachievers*. Some perfectionists avoid taking on certain tasks with the attitude "I can't do it perfectly, so why even bother trying?" This looks like procrastination or avoidance. Other times, we can see this attitude in people who are stuck in jobs that are way below their potential because they're afraid of "failing" at a higher level. And think of the defeatist attitude at play for those who, for example, have not had lasting results losing weight. Many have asked themselves: "Why bother exercising when I can't keep the weight off?"

> *"Perfectionism is not a quest for the best. It is a pursuit of the worst in ourselves, the part that tells us that nothing we do will ever be good enough—that we should try again."*
>
> —JULIA CAMERON, AUTHOR OF *THE ARTIST'S WAY*

THE IMPACT ON OUR LIVES

Perfectionism is a dominant mind-set that influences how you think, feel, and act. Within the field of psychology research, various distinctions have been made in an attempt to classify subtypes of perfectionism. In both my clinical practice and my personal life, I've found it more helpful to examine what perfectionism looks like in the real world and the toll it takes on our lives.

Perfectionism plays a role in *psychological wellness*. A perfectionist tends to be very motivated and driven. To an outsider, perfectionists often look happy, optimistic, and upbeat. On a deeper level, they tend to experience an incredible amount of internal stress, which can lead to depression, anxiety, anger, shame, helplessness, and in rare cases even suicidal behaviors.

We can see the worrisome impact on *physical health*. While some people are diligent about exercise and smart eating, others may push these potentially healthy habits to less than healthy extremes. These can range from frequently worrying about the food they eat to full-blown eating disorders. The "why bother even trying" attitude can also contribute to obesity. And then there are the folks who, ironically, delay going to the doctor because they aren't in perfect health. This mind-set keeps them from getting the help they need.

With the increase in stress associated with perfectionism can come stress-related issues, such as sleep problems, increased stress hormones, headaches, or other chronic pain. Perfectionists are also at increased risk for substance abuse. (Think about this the next time you read about a movie star who seemed to have had it all and yet died of a drug overdose.)

Within *relationships*, perfectionists tend to be doers, especially with noticeable actions like helping out a friend in need or hosting the family holiday meal. They are often very giving, sometimes to the extent of putting the needs of others before their own health or fun. This tendency to focus on accomplishments can often strain relationships, for example when the "doer" misses his daughter's soccer match or arrives late, again, to family gatherings. Loved ones can often feel they've received the short end of the stick compared to the time and energy the perfectionist prioritizes elsewhere.

In a significant relationship, perfectionism can impede intimacy. Perhaps a woman shies away from sex because she doesn't have the "perfect" body. Or she may be preoccupied, thinking things like "You want to have sex even though the dishes haven't been done yet?!" Needless to say, it's tough to be emotionally close to someone with a perfectionist frame of mind. And that sometimes can mean being lonely. Many fear that others will see their "imperfections," and so they are reluctant to really let someone else into their lives.

A perfectionist will often project her own high standards onto others, such as the wife who nitpicks her husband for not doing a load of laundry despite the fact that he vacuumed the entire house to surprise her. So-called bridezillas are often born from perfectionism. Unfortunately, insisting that every aspect of one's wedding be impeccable can alienate friends and family.

Another form is *parental perfectionism*. Consider the new mom who won't let anyone else, even the child's father, do anything for the baby for fear he or she will do it "wrong." Or the dad who pushes his child to excel at sports, even at the cost of the kid just being a kid and having fun. Children may feel consistently judged and shamed by the negative scrutiny of a perfectionist mom or dad. Sadly, they may feel they can never measure up, that they're never good enough.

We often see *perfectionism in the realm of work*, whether that's defined as a traditional job, being a student, or managing the household. In this realm the perfectionist is the hardworking type who responds to emails at two in the morning *and* is the first to arrive at the office. Or the "controlling manager" who won't (or can't) delegate responsibilities despite being overwhelmed by work. Or, even if he does divvy up some tasks, he still micromanages his team, watching their every move.

Many perfectionists have trouble completing tasks. I see this often when coaching entrepreneurs and small-business owners, some of whom don't want to publish their website, circulate their article, or give a business presentation for fear their work won't be perfect.

As a result, perfectionists tend to be rigid in their approach to doing things—a trait a majority of business leaders and managers do not welcome. Instead, they are more likely to prefer having flexible people on their teams, the kind of person who is ready to make adjustments and exceptions when appropriate.

Another difficulty in completing projects derives from the decreased mental functioning—such as difficulty thinking outside the box or writer's block—resulting from the stress of constantly trying to be perfect. Indeed, the stress of the overworking self-editor can make it easier to give up than to persevere.

Within the home or office, some perfectionists require a **tidy environment**. Many are detail-oriented and extremely well organized (even their junk drawer has labeled compartments!). Worse yet, they can get almost insanely upset if anything is out of place.

Perfectionism can also affect **finances**. Many incredibly wealthy individuals (CEOs, movie stars, professional athletes) are perfectionists, as are the highly paid who don't make the *Forbes* wealthiest list. I've seen a lot of perfectionism among those with great wealth. There is often a sense that, despite having many millions of dollars, those millions are just not enough. But perfectionism is not exclusive to the well-off. On the other end of the spectrum, perfectionist procrastination, discouragement, and defeatist attitudes can result in difficulty making ends meet.

Because they tend to **value productivity over fun**, it's not uncommon to hear perfectionists say, "I haven't taken a vacation in years." And when they do take some time off, even if just for a few hours, they tend to stress about everything they think they "should" be doing.

With a life purpose focused on not failing, perfectionists often miss out on a greater sense of *spiritual meaning*. In getting bogged down with getting the details "right," they may forget the big picture of what is truly important to them. As a result, while many perfectionists may look like they have it all, on a deeper level they often feel they are really missing something. To such people, a sense of "Is this all there is in life?" often prevails.

WHAT PERFECTIONISM IS NOT

Let's take a moment to differentiate perfectionism from other traits or conditions often confused with it.

It's not excellence. Having a goal of perfection is not a problem in and of itself. In many cases, it makes sense to go for the gold. Perfectionists strive for excellence, which can be a very positive attribute. Where problems arise is perfectionists' attitude when 100-percent excellence is not achieved.

Perfectionists often personalize an "imperfect" result, equating it with their self-worth: "I am not good enough." For example, research has shown that, despite being the second best in their sport in the *entire world*, silver medalists exhibit a happiness level of about 4.8 on a 10-point scale, with 1 being "agony" and 10 being "ecstasy."

Not succeeding 100 percent 100 percent of the time does not make you a failure. It *does* make you human. It is important to distinguish between a healthy desire for excellence and a stressful, relentless need for perfection. The following scenario exemplifies what I mean.

"Hi," I said to my new client as I extended my hand to shake his. "I'm Dr. Elizabeth Lombardo. Please feel free to call me Elizabeth."

When I introduce myself to clients, I use my title so they know I have the training; I ask that they call me Elizabeth so they know I am approachable.

"Dr. Sterner," my client replied shortly.

Dr. William Sterner had been referred to me by his medical doctor for issues related to chronic pain. It was clear from this first moment that he wanted nothing to do with me.

"I have to be frank with you," he said as we sat down in my office. "I do not really believe in psychology." When he said the word "psychology" he made quotation marks with his hands, as if to say it was not a real scientific discipline.

As we talked about his problems with chronic pain, it became evident that perfectionism was something he struggled with. William told me about stress at home because his wife had recently decided to go back to school. "She does not keep the house like she used to. She told me she would pick up some groceries last Wednesday and she didn't."

When I brought up the concept of perfectionism, he responded, "Of course everything has to be perfect! I'm a brain surgeon. I can't do a half-assed job when I am operating on someone's brain."

Agreed.

"But," I said, "there's a difference between life-and-death circumstances in the operating room and acting as if every mistake is critical outside the OR."

I continued, "What would life outside of brain surgery be like if you strove for excellence and, when it did not happen, you did not beat yourself or others up about it? If instead you dropped the judgment, figured out what went wrong, and took steps to correct it?"

He glared at me with a what-are-you-talking-about? look on his face.

But, because he had promised his medical doctor to see me for at least four sessions, he agreed to work on his stressful thinking (including his perfectionism).

On our fourth session working together, he came in with a smile. I shook his hand, saying, "Hello Dr. Sterner," and he responded, "Call me William."

As soon as he sat down, he animatedly told me about how his wife had sat him down the day before to say how proud she was of all the changes he was making. By using the strategies in Better Than Perfect that I'm about to share with you, William realized he could strive for excellence and not stress out as much—or stress out those around him. What's more, he had noticed a significant decrease in his level of pain.

"I guess there really is something to this 'psychology,'" he said with a smile.

It's not narcissism. "Narcissism" is a term that seems to be thrown around a lot these days. It is characterized by an inflated sense of self-importance, focus on yourself, and need for admiration from those around you.

Narcissists are egocentric and preoccupied with themselves, their preferences, and their needs. I'm sure you know people like this. The "friend" who incessantly talks about herself, but has no time to hear about your life. The person who skips the line while boarding the plane or entering a concert, pretending not to notice the dozens (or more) who'd been waiting their turn. The neighbor who plays loud music at all hours of the night and then calls the police when your guest parks in front of his house.

> *"I am careful not to confuse excellence with perfection. Excellence I can reach for; perfection is God's business."*
> —MICHAEL J. FOX

Sometimes perfectionists look a bit like narcissists on the outside because of their laser-focus on achieving a task. Their fear of failure and desire to win fuel a competitive nature that can be seen by others as caring only about themselves. Perfectionists' conviction that there is one "right" way—theirs—often comes across as egocentric.

In reality, perfectionists are not (usually) narcissists. They do not lack empathy, which is a key component of narcissism. Unlike narcissists, they do not see themselves as special or act in emotional, dramatic ways.

It's not obsessive-compulsive disorder (OCD). I often hear people using the term "OCD" to describe perfectionism. In reality, the two traits are quite different.

OCD is an anxiety disorder characterized by obsessions (seemingly uncontrollable fearful thoughts) and compulsions (repetitive behaviors geared at helping reduce these obsessions). An example would be people whose fear of getting sick from germs (obsession) brings them to repeatedly wash their hands (compulsion). Or a superstitious fear that something bad will happen (obsession) brings you to count to one hundred, or to impeccably arrange items around you (compulsion).

OCD can be debilitating, significantly affecting your emotional wellness and/or quality of life in work, health, and relationships. I once had a client who sterilized the entire bathroom (tub, toilet, sink, floors) every night. It took over two hours!

It's true that perfectionists also have anxiety regarding their fear of failure, and they may take steps to address those fears. But, while some perfectionists also suffer from OCD, the two conditions are distinct issues.

It's not spiritual perfectionism. There is a huge difference between the perfectionism we're talking about in this book—the notion that "things must be 'perfect' in order for me to feel okay about myself"—and what I will call spiritual perfectionism.

Spiritual perfectionism involves the premise that all that is, is perfect. Here, "perfect" refers to acceptance of reality on a higher, more spiritual level. Ideals such as "everything happens for a reason," "you are a perfect creation," and "divine perfection" are included in this concept.

Cultivating your spiritual beliefs is an important component of a Better Than Perfect life. But, whether or not you buy into the concept that you are already perfect in a very true and tangible way, it is important to understand the difference between spiritual perfectionism and the perfectionism we are talking about here.

GLOBAL VERSUS LOCAL

Some perfectionists exhibit these traits globally in all (or at least most) facets of their lives.

Others experience perfectionism in specific areas, such as:

- Work

- School

- "Free" time

- Cleaning/organizing

- Relationships

- Physical appearance

- Weight

- Eating

- Fitness

- Other health issues

- Sports

- Finances

- Worldview

Where do you see perfectionism showing up in your life?

WHAT'S NEXT?

While there's evidence that perfectionism has a biological basis, this way of viewing and interacting in the world is fueled by the internal dialogue in a person's mind. As a result, research shows that perfectionism can be altered by means of psychological approaches. In fact, the strategies presented here are based on cognitive behavioral principles. We will address both the thoughts and the behaviors that result in perfectionist patterns, as well as discuss how to change them so they are more helpful to you.

"In nature, nothing is perfect and everything is perfect. Trees can be contorted, bent in weird ways, and they're still beautiful."
—ALICE WALKER

In the next chapter, "Are You a Perfectionist?," there is an assessment you can take to see how much perfectionism plays a role in your life. This is a fun way to look at what is going on with you, as well as a great tool to share with others.

In Chapter 3 we'll look at "The Price and Profits of Perfectionism." This chapter will help you explore what is and is not working for you when it comes to perfectionism. Remember, I am not suggesting that you give up who you are or anything that is truly enhancing your life. This chapter will help you better understand both how to keep what's working well and what you may want to alter. Then, in Chapter 4, "Fear Versus Passion," we'll examine the liabilities of operating out of fear, and the potential advantages of instead using passion as one's driving force.

That brings us to Part Two, the Better Than Perfect program: 7 Strategies to Crush Your Inner Critic and Create a Life You Love. These are based on research-supported cognitive behavioral therapy as well as my own personal and clinical experiences. These guidelines have helped me and so many of my clients find greater joy, satisfaction, control, balance, and success in our lives. The seven steps, listed below, spell PERFECT.

Postmortem Your Past

Evaluate Your Expectations

Reinforce New Roads

Fail Forward

Eliminate Extremes

Create, Don't Compare

Transcend

Each chapter in Part Two explores a separate program strategy and then provides Action Steps you can take to create the life you deserve. Most of the actions are quick and easy, but don't let that fool you. They are very powerful.

Finally, the Epilogue will help you assess where you are in the program, what attitudes or fears may be holding you back, and how to overcome them. It will also remind you that you are already Better Than Perfect and can continue to make incredible changes in your life.

And if you have questions—while reading this book or any other time—please reach out. Feel free to post a comment or question on my Facebook page: www.facebook.com/Dr.Elizabeth.Lombardo.

You are *not* in this alone. You have me and many others in the Better Than Perfect community here to help you flourish in ways you may never have imagined possible. Now, let's jump right in. See you on the next page!

CHAPTER 2

Are You a Perfectionist?

"If the world were perfect, it wouldn't be."
—YOGI BERRA

Now let's get a better sense of the degree to which perfectionism shows up in your life. To help you do that, I've designed the self-scoring quiz below. Before you read on, I encourage you to take a few moments to complete it.

Relax! There are no right or wrong answers. Our only goal is to pinpoint your perfectionist "hot buttons" so we can zero in on them.

You can either take the quiz on paper or complete it online—whatever works best for you. If you prefer taking it online, just go to www.ElizabethLombardo.com/BetterThanPerfect. Let's get started.

EXERCISE: PERFECTIONIST SELF-ASSESSMENT

On a scale from 1 to 4, rate how much you agree with each statement:

4 = ALL THE TIME
3 = SOMETIMES
2 = RARELY
1 = NEVER

		ALL THE TIME (4)	SOMETIMES (3)	RARELY (2)	NEVER (1)
1.	People often say I have "unrealistic expectations."				
2.	I tend to judge myself by what I accomplish.				
3.	I often miss out on enjoyable and exciting events because I am working so hard.				
4.	I often beat myself up mentally.				
5.	I consistently minimize my accomplishments, but secretly wish other people would make a bigger deal about them.				
6.	I pretty much live by the motto, "If you can't do something right (perfectly), why bother doing it at all?"				
7.	I believe nothing good comes from mistakes.				
8.	I hate it when I don't get everything right the first time.				
9.	I have no free time. ▶				

	ALL THE TIME (4)	SOMETIMES (3)	RARELY (2)	NEVER (1)
10. I believe no achievement is ever enough.				
11. I don't like it when other people don't do things my way.				
12. I can't trust others to do as good a job as I would, so I end up doing a lot of other people's work.				
13. I am sometimes so afraid of failing that I don't even start.				
14. I like being prepared for whatever may happen.				
15. I often feel stressed out and tense when it comes to getting things done.				
16. When I achieve a goal, I enjoy the victory only for a short time before going on to the next project.				
17. I have trouble making decisions.				
18. I can be extremely detail-oriented.				
19. I have pretty demanding standards for myself and those around me.				
20. I try to prevent failing at all costs.				
21. I tend to think in absolutes. If I am on a diet and eat one cookie, I'll keep eating more since I've already ruined my diet. ▶				

	ALL THE TIME (4)	SOMETIMES (3)	RARELY (2)	NEVER (1)
22. If I think about it, I realize I use the word "should" quite often.				
23. Enjoying myself or having fun is okay, but only after I finish all my work.				
24. My self-confidence is dependent on my accomplishments and/or how others react to what I do.				
25. I tend to replay over and over what I've screwed up. I usually don't focus on what I did well.				
26. I procrastinate or avoid situations that I think I will not be good in.				
27. I have trouble finishing projects because there's always something more I can do to make it better.				
28. I frequently make lists.				
29. I like being organized and have trouble starting something new if everything is not well organized and in its place.				
30. I am very competitive.				

Scoring: Add up your total points and use the scoring system below to help you figure out where you are on the perfectionist spectrum.

30: No perfectionism here. That said, continue reading so you can better understand and interact with the perfectionists in your life. Then give this book to someone you know who really needs it.

31–60: You have some perfectionist qualities that may be hindering your true self, but they are not overbearing. You also exhibit a good grasp of the skills in the Better Than Perfect program. Use this book to help polish and boost these skills to help you, your relationships, your work, and your life flourish even more.

61–90: You figured you had some perfectionist qualities, but didn't realize how much they were affecting your life until you read over the statements above. Whether you call it perfectionism or something else, these characteristics are preventing the true you from shining through. Go through this book, apply the concepts, and enjoy the benefits they bring to your life.

91–119: Perfectionist tendencies are causing some real issues in your life. Your happiness, self-esteem, physical health, relationships, work, finances, fun, and sense of fulfillment are not where you want them to be. Never fear. My Better Than Perfect plan will help you keep what's working for you and change the rest. Begin applying the Better Than Perfect strategies and target specific areas, such as work or your personal relationships.

120: You scored "perfectly" on the perfectionist quiz. (This may not have been an exam where you wanted to get 100 percent!) Do not stop. Immediately turn the page, keep reading. Start applying these techniques to specific high-impact areas, such as work or your personal relationships. You deserve happiness and satisfaction, you deserve to be kinder to yourself, and you deserve to live a life that is Better Than Perfect.

CHAPTER 3

The Price and Profits of Perfectionism

The smell of cigarettes hit my nose way before I met Andrew in the waiting room. When he'd called to set up an appointment the week before, he'd said he wanted our session to focus on smoking cessation.

Once Andrew was sitting in my office, I asked him, "So, what is good about smoking?"

"Good?" he asked, with an are-you-crazy? look on his face. "What do you mean 'good'? Nothing is good about smoking. It causes lung cancer, it's ridiculously expensive, and it stinks."

While all of those statements are true, I knew there was something more. "So why do you smoke?" I asked.

"Because I am addicted," Andrew replied.

"You told me on the phone last week that nicotine replacements have not worked in the past. So it must be more than your body craving nicotine."

"Well . . . smoking helps me relax, especially during a stressful day." The conversation went on, with Andrew talking about all of the "good" he found in smoking.

Please, no tweets suggesting I'm collaborating with a tobacco company! In the scenario above I'm certainly not saying that smoking is "good." And by no means am I recommending that you go buy a pack of cigarettes in order to relax! Smoking can kill you as well as those around you. One in five deaths can be linked to smoking, and it can lead to numerous illnesses, including heart disease, stroke, and cancer.

So why did I share this dialogue with you? Because it highlights the reality that even bad habits have some "good" in them—at least in the mind of the person doing them. It also underscores the fact that, in order to change a habit, you need to find other sources to give you the "good" the habit offers. Otherwise, the pull of the "benefits" you get from your old habit will continue to exert power, and you will quickly find yourself slipping back into your old ways.

This is a key point when it comes to changing any behavior pattern—and one that's usually overlooked. Have you ever been angry with yourself for making a commitment to change something, such as your weight or your daily alcohol consumption, only to revert back to your old ways at some point? The problem wasn't that you were weak or a loser or even destined to have that habit forever. You didn't need more willpower per se. What you needed instead was to get the benefits the habit provides in more healthy and helpful ways.

Perfectionist tendencies are, in a sense, habits: a habitual way of thinking, interacting with the world around you, and viewing yourself and others. Certainly there are some positive aspects of perfectionism. In fact, when I work with clients, the thought of changing their perfectionist inclinations often scares the heck out of them. In such moments they're focusing on the positives, such as previous accomplishments and striving for success, without considering the heavy price they often pay in their relentless drive to pursue desired goals.

Let's focus on what's helpful—the "good"—and what's not so helpful. This is an important conversation to have whenever you want to make any change in your life. Too often, when we are in "change mode," we limit our focus to only one side of the pro/con equation without accounting for all the variables. But this narrow approach can prevent us from taking advantage of all the motivational incentives we need both to put ourselves firmly on the road to change and to stay the course.

To get a better sense of what I mean, consider the smoking example above. Initially, most smokers tend to focus on the reasons they want to quit—the "con" part of the equation—just as Andrew did. As time progresses, however, the positives of smoking—the "pro" part—such as stress relief or appetite suppression, come to the forefront and may reassert themselves, often causing a relapse. But by finding new ways to address the desired goals, such as stress relief, you can take away the "need" to smoke.

We are going to explore ways to keep what truly is working for you and to replace what isn't. The result? Joy, satisfaction, prosperity, and success can be yours in ways you never imagined.

LOOK AT THE BIG PICTURE

As I mentioned, when exploring how something affects our lives, it's important to take a comprehensive look at both the price and payoff involved. In my work with clients, I've found that helping them see the "big picture" is the most effective first step on the road to creating real change and transformation in their lives. To do this, let's look at what I call the Pros and Cons of the Present Versus Change (PCPC).

The table below illustrates this visually.

TEMPLATE: PROS AND CONS OF THE PRESENT VERSUS CHANGE (PCPC)

	PROS	CONS
PRESENT	A	B
CHANGE	C	D

In this diagram, Section A represents the "pros" or benefits provided by one's current way of thinking and behaving. Section B depicts the "cons" or costs of these current behaviors. Section C illustrates the potential benefits of changing how one currently thinks and acts. Finally, Section D portrays the "cons" or possible costs of those changes.

Using Andrew's example from the previous page, here is a simplified version:

SAMPLE: DETAIL FROM ANDREW'S PCPC

	PROS	CONS
PRESENT	• Helps me relax • Something I do with my friends	• My girlfriend said she will leave me if I keep smoking • Endangers my health
CHANGE	• My girlfriend won't leave me • My clothes and house will smell much better	• I might feel stressed and anxious • I might gain weight

In the above example, we looked at only a small part of Andrew's life. For you, though, we want to be more comprehensive. To do that, within each of these boxes, we want to look at the pros and cons of perfectionism in seven major areas:

- *Psychological Wellness:* How does this behavior affect you emotionally and mentally?

- *Physical Health:* How does it affect your body and physical well-being?

- *Relationships:* How does it affect relationships with your significant other, family, friends, and coworkers?

- *Work:* How does it affect your work? Here, "work" is defined in the broad sense of how you spend your days. This may be work in a more traditional sense, work at home (such as a stay-at-home parent or someone who works from home), going to school, or looking for a job.

- *Financial:* How does it affect how much money comes in and goes out? How does it influence your relationship with money?

- *Fun:* How does it affect the fun and enjoyment you have in your life? (I must admit I never used to include this category when working with clients. I always focused on the other components and never really considered assessing their fun factor. Why? Because my own perfectionism tended to minimize the importance of this quality. And yet, isn't fun an important part of life?)

- *Spiritual Health:* How does it help boost your spiritual energy? This assessment goes beyond religion (although that may be included here) to encompass your values and beliefs about your purpose in life. Yes, I admit, this may seem like "heavy" stuff, but it's also very important. Spiritual health can lead to better physical health, a sense of fulfillment, decisiveness, and even more success.

These categories are certainly not mutually exclusive. These seven components are often interrelated. For example, relationships at work can be included in the relationship and/or work category. What's more, relationships can affect happiness. Work can influence finances. Physical health can influence fun. The goal is not to get hung up on which category something goes in. (I know that can be tough for some perfectionists.) The purpose of using these divisions is to gain a comprehensive view of how your life is being affected by your perfectionist traits—and what will improve if you change.

When thinking about each category, consider issues you're currently experiencing as a result of your drive to be perfect, as well as possible short-term and long-term consequences. For example, the overwhelming stress often associated with perfectionism may not be impacting your health now, but research shows it may in the future (through the increased risk for illness and even earlier death).

"People rarely succeed unless they have fun in what they are doing."
—DALE CARNEGIE

SECTION A: THE PROS OF PERFECTIONISM

Let's start with the benefits of your current approach. What do you gain from perfectionism?

EXERCISE: THE PROS OF PERFECTIONISM

In the list below, check off or highlight any of the benefits that particularly resonate with you. Feel free to add some of your own.

Psychological Wellness
- ☐ I feel good about myself when I do something others can't easily do.
- ☐ It feels good to get stuff done.
- ☐ I feel engaged in the tasks in my life.
- ☐ I like to be appreciated for my efforts.
- ☐ _____
- ☐ _____

▶

Physical Health

- ☐ My strict health regimen (eating and/or exercising) makes my body look better.
- ☐ People comment on how "good" I am with my eating and/or exercise regimens.
- ☐ _____
- ☐ _____

Relationships

- ☐ I help out my friends; they can always count on me.
- ☐ I am modeling for my children the importance of hard work.
- ☐ When I throw a party, my friends always have fun.
- ☐ _____
- ☐ _____

Work

- ☐ I can be productive.
- ☐ I work long hours.
- ☐ I like things to be done well—and no one does them as well as I do.
- ☐ I get rewarded for my hard work.
- ☐ I like being prepared for whatever may happen.
- ☐ I like admiring what I create.
- ☐ I appreciate excellent work.
- ☐ I love being efficient.
- ☐ It feels good to be organized.
- ☐ I like being at the top of my company/business/class.
- ☐ I get good grades/evaluations.
- ☐ My supervisor often gives me tough projects because she knows I will do a good job.
- ☐ I'm careful to avoid the negative consequences some coworkers receive because of their lack of discipline.
- ☐ _____
- ☐ _____

▶

Financial

- ☐ Because I work so hard, I make pretty good money.
- ☐ My studies/hard work will bring me more money in the future.
- ☐ I am disciplined with my spending.
- ☐ _____
- ☐ _____

Fun

- ☐ My hard work is paid well, so I get to go on fun trips.
- ☐ I feel I've earned my fun because I work so hard.
- ☐ I can afford to buy fun stuff (like the newest gadget as soon as it comes out).
- ☐ _____
- ☐ _____

Spiritual Health

- ☐ I go to church every Sunday.
- ☐ Perseverance and integrity are important values to me.
- ☐ _____
- ☐ _____

SECTION B: THE PRICE OF PERFECTIONISM

Now that we've identified some beneficial components of perfectionism, let's look at some of the costs associated with this worldview.

EXERCISE: THE PRICE OF PERFECTIONISM

Again, check off or highlight any items in the list below that hit close to home. Feel free to add some of your own as well.

Psychological Wellness

- ☐ My stress level is through the roof.
- ☐ I am constantly beating myself up.
- ☐ I struggle with depression.

▶

- [ ] I often feel anxious.
- [ ] I worry a lot.
- [ ] It is hard to let go of the past.
- [ ] I have a lot of shame (even if I don't want to admit it).
- [ ] I feel guilty.
- [ ] I often feel anger or frustration.
- [ ] I judge myself a lot.
- [ ] I have conditional love for myself.
- [ ] I often feel resentful toward others.
- [ ] I never truly feel satisfied with what I've done.
- [ ] _____
- [ ] _____

Physical Health

- [ ] If I were really honest with myself, I would acknowledge that my eating is probably too restrictive.
- [ ] Sometimes, after I don't let myself eat something, I later binge eat.
- [ ] Sometimes when I eat something "bad" for me, I keep eating, thinking "I already screwed up, might as well eat more."
- [ ] Exercise takes up a lot of my time.
- [ ] I exercise even when I am sick.
- [ ] I don't exercise at all because I don't have time.
- [ ] I have a horrible time getting to sleep.
- [ ] I often wake up early and can't fall back asleep.
- [ ] I haven't had eight hours of sleep in a long time.
- [ ] I usually have to take a pill in order to sleep.
- [ ] I feel exhausted.
- [ ] My muscles are tense.
- [ ] I have chronic pain.
- [ ] I have frequent tension headaches.
- [ ] I consistently feel on the edge.
- [ ] I have a lot of stomach/GI issues.
- [ ] I feel worn-out.
- [ ] I tend to get sick a lot.

▶

☐ While I may be okay now, research shows that high levels of stress can lead to lots of health problems down the road.

☐ Because of my high levels of stress, I have an increased risk for early death. (Scary but true!)

☐ _____

☐ _____

Relationships

☐ I don't spend as much time with my friends or family as I would like to.

☐ I feel isolated.

☐ My significant other and I rarely have time for just the two of us to enjoy together.

☐ My family gets upset with me because I am always working.

☐ I find it hard to forgive people and move on.

☐ When I correct others, they get upset or annoyed.

☐ I place high demands on the people in my life.

☐ I get more angry and frustrated with my loved ones than I want to.

☐ I tend to judge others, including those closest to me.

☐ I am too tired to spend time with my family and friends.

☐ Even when I am physically with friends and family, my mind is usually elsewhere, so I miss out on what they are saying and really enjoying my time with them.

☐ My frequent need for assurance is taxing to those around me.

☐ My relationships in the long term could be really hurt by the way I act now.

☐ _____

☐ _____

Work

☐ I put relentless pressure on myself (and others) to do better and better.

☐ I often feel as if my best efforts aren't good enough.

☐ I tend to micromanage others, which gives me a lot more work.

☐ I consistently feel like a failure.

☐ Despite any successes, I feel as if I have to keep working, rather than sit back and appreciate what I have done.

▶

☐ I often procrastinate.

☐ It takes me a really long time to finish a task.

☐ I check and recheck my work (and sometimes others'). This takes time and energy I don't really have.

☐ I am indecisive because I am fearful I will make a mistake.

☐ I avoid certain situations because I'm afraid I'll fail.

☐ I feel as if I have to keep proving myself to others at work—and that is exhausting.

☐ I am at risk for serious burnout.

☐ I have difficulty thinking "outside the box."

☐ _____

☐ _____

Financial

☐ Although I make pretty good money, it never seems to be enough.

☐ My avoidance and procrastination cause me to make less money.

☐ Because I want to feel and look successful, I tend to spend a lot of money (on clothes, status symbols like the latest car or iPad).

☐ I never feel as if I have enough money.

☐ _____

☐ _____

Fun

☐ I don't allow myself to have fun until my work is done—which is hardly ever.

☐ Fun is not a consistent part of my everyday life.

☐ I can rarely find time to have fun and relax with my family.

☐ My significant other and I don't take time to do something just for fun very often.

☐ I have fun at work, but rarely just for the sake of fun.

☐ _____

☐ _____

Spiritual Health

☐ I have no time to consider my purpose in life.

☐ Even thinking about finding meaning in life stresses me out.

▶

□ My spiritual health is not a priority to me, even though I would like it to be.

□ I don't really know what my spiritual beliefs are.

□ I do not take time to focus on my spirituality.

□ _____

□ _____

SECTION C: THE PROS OF CHANGE

Now let's look at how changing perfectionistic thinking and acting might be beneficial to you.

EXERCISE: THE PROS OF CHANGE

While you can't *know* how things would be different if you changed your perfectionistic thinking, use the following checklist to consider possible advantages you might achieve within each of these seven categories. Again, feel free to add some of your own.

Psychological Wellness

□ I'd have less stress—*that* would be amazing!

□ I'd feel happier.

□ I'd feel more satisfied with my life.

□ I wouldn't be depressed all the time.

□ I'd have more self-confidence.

□ I'd have less worry and anxiety.

□ I'd have more peace of mind.

□ I'd have less shame and guilt.

□ I'd be less angry and frustrated with myself and others.

□ I'd feel much better about myself.

□ I'd feel more joy.

□ _____

□ _____

▶

Physical Health

- ☐ I'd sleep better.
- ☐ I'd have less tension in my body.
- ☐ I'd have less illness.
- ☐ I'd be more likely to live longer.
- ☐ I'd suffer fewer stomach/GI issues.
- ☐ I'd have less pain.
- ☐ I'd be healthier.
- ☐ _____
- ☐ _____

Relationships

- ☐ I'd be closer with my family.
- ☐ I'd have a closer and deeper relationship with my significant other.
- ☐ I'd be closer with my friends.
- ☐ I'd take the pressure off my loved ones to be "perfect."
- ☐ My loved ones would feel more love from me.
- ☐ I'd be more mindful and fully present when I'm around the people I love.
- ☐ I'd enjoy deeper connections.
- ☐ I'd make new friends.
- ☐ I'd stop spending time with negative people just because I think I "should."
- ☐ I'd be more forgiving.
- ☐ I'd be more easygoing, especially with the little things.
- ☐ I'd get along better with the people around me.
- ☐ _____
- ☐ _____

Work

- ☐ I'd stop overextending myself.
- ☐ I'd learn to say no and be okay with it.
- ☐ I'd be more decisive.
- ☐ I'd work fewer hours.
- ☐ I'd be more productive.
- ☐ I'd have greater creativity and ingenuity.
- ☐ I'd enjoy work more.

▶

☐ I'd feel more fulfilled from my work.

☐ I'd be less mentally exhausted at the end of the day.

☐ I'd feel more satisfied with my work.

☐ _____

☐ _____

Financial

☐ I may make more money if I accept more lucrative challenges.

☐ I'd spend less money because I wouldn't need to buy stuff in order to feel good about myself.

☐ I'd have a better relationship with money. Instead of focusing on thinking there's never enough, I would concentrate on being grateful for what I have.

☐ _____

☐ _____

Fun

☐ I'd give myself permission to have fun.

☐ I'd have a lot more time to relax and have fun.

☐ I'd be able to enjoy what I already have.

☐ I'd be more playful with my loved ones.

☐ Having fun would actually be more of a priority in my life.

☐ _____

☐ _____

Spiritual Health

☐ I'd explore my beliefs more.

☐ I'd feel more fulfilled.

☐ I'd apply my values more, which will help me have more joy.

☐ I'd have greater peace of mind.

☐ _____

☐ _____

Did any of these surprise you? Can you imagine a life in which you experience these benefits? What would your outlook and energy level be if these benefits were yours? Write down your thoughts.

_____

_____

_____

_____

_____

_____

SECTION D: THE CONS OF CHANGE

Now, let's look at the potential downsides of changing. This is an important step: if we do not address these items, change is unlikely to be sustained.

EXERCISE: THE CONS OF CHANGE

Psychological Wellness

- ☐ I don't like the unknown. It makes me feel anxious.
- ☐ I'm not sure how I will define myself.
- ☐ I am worried it won't work.
- ☐ What if I can't do it?
- ☐ I may not feel as important or significant.
- ☐ My stress could go up as I am trying this change.
- ☐ _____
- ☐ _____

Physical Health

- ☐ What if my health doesn't get better immediately?
- ☐ I may gain weight if I am not as stringent with my eating or exercise.
- ☐ I may not be as regimented with my vitamins and medications.
- ☐ I may not care about my health as much.
- ☐ _____
- ☐ _____

Relationships

- ☐ My friends and family might not like the new me.
- ☐ My family may feel I am not taking as much care of them.
- ☐ If I don't put as much pressure on my children to succeed, they may fail or not excel as much.
- ☐ _____
- ☐ _____

Work

- ☐ I might become lazy.
- ☐ The quality of my work may diminish.
- ☐ My coworkers may not like the new me.
- ☐ My supervisors may think I am slacking off.
- ☐ If I am doing less work my colleagues or staff will resent the additional work they'd have to do.
- ☐ Or: if I stop procrastinating as much I might end up with more work.

▶

☐ I might get into more stressful situations that I have been avoiding because of my perfectionism.

☐ _____

☐ _____

Financial

☐ I could make less money.

☐ I may worry more about money.

☐ I may not be able to save enough.

☐ _____

☐ _____

Fun

☐ I might not be able to afford the fun things I do now.

☐ I might feel I don't deserve to have fun because I haven't "earned" it.

☐ _____

☐ _____

Spiritual Health

☐ I won't feel like the real me.

☐ I might start questioning my beliefs.

☐ _____

☐ _____

Okay, now it's time for you to complete the following PCPC table as it relates to your personal life. Use the examples from above that are relevant to you. Also feel free to add your own important factors from your personal or work life. You are the expert on you. Don't judge yourself as you write. Try not to filter or minimize either the helpful or the not-so-helpful items. Be as honest with yourself as you can. Your honesty will be crucial to finding the happiness and success that you want and deserve!

EXERCISE: YOUR PROS AND CONS OF THE PRESENT VERSUS CHANGE (PCPC)

Fill out your own Pros and Cons of the Present Versus Change (PCPC) chart with as much information as you can. Here's a model to get you started.

CATEGORIES TO CONSIDER: Psychological Wellness, Physical Health, Relationships, Work, Financial, Fun, and Spiritual Health

CATEGORY			PROS	CONS
	Present		A	B
	Change		C	D

Now that you've completed your chart, consider some of your answers.

What surprises you the most?

_____

_____

_____

▶

What excites you the most?

_____

_____

_____

What scares you the most?

_____

_____

_____

One client told me she was afraid of failing. "I have been like this for as long as I can remember. How can I become someone else? Wouldn't that make me feel like a fake? What if it doesn't work? What if I put all this time and energy into making changes and things get worse?"

To address her fear of not being able to change, I offered this analogy: "Before you learned to ride a bicycle, you probably were off balance when you sat on the seat. You were not sure how much to lean to the left or tilt to the right in order to stay upright. When you were trying to ride the bike, all of your attention was probably focused on staying upright.

"Now, though, riding a bike comes naturally to you—even if you haven't done it for a while. You hardly even think about how to sit on it without falling over. It has become automatic.

"Learning to behave in nonperfectionist ways will be like riding a bike. It may seem awkward at first. But the more you do it, the easier and more automatic it becomes."

REFRAMING THE PROS OF PERFECTIONISM

Now we want to address the items you charted in your PCPC table. In the next steps we'll look specifically at the concerns in Section A: "The Pros of Perfectionism," and Section D: "The Cons of Change." For every benefit of keeping your old behavior in place, we'll want to identify new, more appealing benefits to changing. Take a look at the examples below.

CATEGORY	SECTION A: THE PROS OF PERFECTIONISM OLD THOUGHTS	WAYS TO REFRAME THE SUPPOSED BENEFITS OF PERFECTIONISM NEW THOUGHTS
Psychological Wellness	I feel good about myself when I do something that others cannot easily do.	I can feel good about myself by accomplishing things and find additional confidence-boosters that don't require excessive work and stress.
Psychological Wellness	It feels good to get stuff done.	I can still get stuff done, just without the excessive stress.
Physical Health	My strict health regimen (eating and/or exercising) makes my body look better.	I don't need to be all or nothing. I can eat and exercise in healthy ways without going to extremes.
Work	I can be efficient and productive.	I can still be efficient and productive—maybe even more so—if I schedule my time wisely and take breaks to restore my mental and physical energy.

Now it's your turn.

EXERCISE: REFRAMING THE PROS OF PERFECTIONISM

Review the concerns you listed in Section A: "The Pros of Perfectionism" of your PCPC chart. For each perfectionism you listed in Section A, identify a new way to achieve a similar or even better benefit.

CATEGORIES TO CONSIDER: Psychological Wellness, Physical Health, Relationships, Work, Financial, Fun, and Spiritual Health

CATEGORY	SECTION A: THE PROS OF PERFECTIONISM OLD THOUGHTS	WAYS TO REFRAME THE SUPPOSED BENEFITS OF PERFECTIONISM NEW THOUGHTS

REFRAMING THE CONS OF CHANGE

Now we're going to look at ways you can overcome your fears about changing. This involves identifying ways to calm each fear that holds you back so you can benefit from the change you want to make. Below are some examples.

CATEGORY	SECTION D: THE CONS OF CHANGE OLD THOUGHTS	REFRAMING THE CONS OF CHANGE NEW THOUGHTS
Psychological Wellness	I don't like the unknown. It makes me feel anxious.	The more I do it, the more comfortable I'll feel acting in a way that is ultimately more helpful to me.
Physical Health	I may gain weight if I am not as stringent with my eating or exercise.	My body will be more healthy as I exercise and make healthy eating choices—without going to extremes.
Relationships	My friends and family might not like the new me.	My loved ones will appreciate that I'm happier, which will help us be closer.
Work	The quality of my work may diminish.	I may be even more productive and creative when my inner critic is not shouting at me.

Now it's your turn.

EXERCISE: REFRAMING THE CONS OF CHANGE

Review the fears you listed in Section D: "The Cons of Change." For each fear, identify a way to assuage that fear so you can benefit from the change you want to make.

CATEGORIES TO CONSIDER: Psychological Wellness, Physical Health, Relationships, Work, Financial, Fun, and Spiritual Health

CATEGORY	SECTION D: THE CONS OF CHANGE OLD THOUGHTS	WAYS TO REFRAME THE SUPPOSED CONS OF CHANGE NEW THOUGHTS

Now that we know the benefits of making changes in your perfectionism, let's jump into transforming your life! Are you ready to live a Better Than Perfect life?

CHAPTER 4

Fear Versus Passion

W HAT'S YOUR PREDOMINANT driver: fear or passion? Put another way, what motivates you more: wanting to minimize a feared outcome, or wanting to maximize a desired outcome? For example, if you were asked to give a speech in front of a couple hundred people, would you be more likely to think:

"I'd better not mess this up and look like a loser."

or

"What a great opportunity to share something I care about with such a big group."

The first response is more fear-based, while the second is more passion-based. In this chapter we're going to look at how these two very different motivators can affect your life in very different ways.

Just as we choose the fuel for our bodies, we get to choose the fuel for our lives: fear or passion.

What drives perfectionists to be "perfect" is fear, especially fear of failure. They'll often go to great lengths to avoid making a mistake or otherwise appearing to others as if they are not good enough. And since they gauge their self-worth against the achievement of specific, often unattainable goals, they consistently feel they've somehow fallen short. That's a tough way to get through your day, isn't it?

When you are fueled by fear, you focus on what you *don't* want. Your goal is to do everything in your power to reduce the possibility of an undesired outcome. You worry about what might happen and take steps to minimize or prevent negative events from occurring. Fear is on the same energetic spectrum as anger, judgment, anxiety, resentment, shame, guilt, jealousy, hatred, and panic. Not the most pleasant experiences.

Just by switching your perspective from one of fear to one of passion—working toward a desired outcome instead of avoiding an unwanted result—you can begin to feel more motivated, engaged, positive, and hopeful. Passion encompasses enthusiasm and excitement for life and exists on an alternate energy spectrum. It includes romantic passion as well as joy, fun, determination, resilience, love, gratitude, and purpose.

When you are fueled by passion, you are motivated by what you *want* to experience rather than by the need to minimize what you *don't* want. We experience passion when we are applying our values and strengths, when we are being our true selves, and when we are taking on challenges that energize us. Your true self is the part of you that can experience contentment and satisfaction and finds meaning in what you do and enjoyment in what life brings.

Remember, I'm your happiness coach. The goal of the Better Than Perfect program is to help you find true and lasting happiness in your life. And, I assure you, using passion as your fuel to get through the day is the shortest path to joy.

Here are some examples of the striking differences between how fear and passion can show up in your life:

SAMPLE: A LIFE OF FEAR OR A LIFE OF PASSION

Relationships	**FEAR:** I can't trust him. What if he cheats on me?! **PASSION:** I choose to focus on the love we have.
Parenting	**FEAR:** My kids need to do well in school or else they will never get into a good college. **PASSION:** I want to help my children cultivate their values and strengths.
Health	**FEAR:** What if this strange feeling is cancer and I die? **PASSION:** I am grateful for all my body does for me and will continue to take steps to be healthy.
Work	**FEAR:** This project is so stressful. I could get fired if I mess it up. **PASSION:** I enjoy using my strengths and collaborating with others to make this an incredible project.
Money	**FEAR:** What if I lose it all? That would be terrible. **PASSION:** I will save some, spend some, and donate some. I am so grateful for the money I have.
Spirit	**FEAR:** What if there is no afterlife? **PASSION:** I choose to believe in life after death. I get strength in prayer. And, hey, if I'm wrong about afterlife, I'll be dead before I find out!

Striking, isn't it? Thoughts and beliefs driven by passion create a totally different view of the world around you, and that fresh, positive perspective creates a completely different life. Whereas a fear-based perspective emphasizes the *potential* for negative or catastrophic consequences, a passion-based perspective focuses on gratitude while cultivating a life that keeps getting better and better.

The beauty is you get to choose which fuel you want to drive your life. You get to choose between being fear-focused and passion-focused. And the difference between living your life fueled with passion and living your life fueled with fear is nothing short of remarkable.

So now that we're on the subject, let's consider: what exactly *is* fear? Fear is a fabrication in our minds—something we are imagining that we don't want to happen. If you hear a crash in the middle of the night and are frightened, it's not *because* of the loud sound, but rather what you *think* the sound might have been caused by—perhaps your pet knocking over something valuable or, worse, someone breaking into your home.

I like to think of fear as an acronym for

Fictitious

Envisioning

Altering

Reality

Fear is fictitious (something made up), envisioning (in your mind), altering (changing) your reality (what is really happening). Just as fictitious stories *can* become true, so can our fears, as depicted in the following scenario.

*During the third year in my psychology training, I was work-
ing in the field of psycho-oncology—helping people who had
cancer. One day I received a consult saying "forty-seven-year-
old female with Stage 4 breast cancer."*

*Turns out, the woman was also a surgical oncologist. So
basically, she regularly operated on people going through
exactly what she was experiencing at that moment.*

*Susan sat in the dimmed therapy room looking down
at her hands, giving off a feeling of defeat. Stage 4 cancer is
extremely serious, but Susan's distress went even deeper than
her poor prognosis.*

*"I felt a lump eleven months ago," she confided. "I knew
it was cancer and I got scared. I know it's stupid—I mean I
know that early detection and treatment can result in better
outcomes. I know that in my head. But I got so scared that I
just ignored it.*

*"My mom died from breast cancer when she was young.
That's why I went to med school—to help people like her.
As soon as I felt the little ball in my breast, I pictured her
last days. She was emaciated. She couldn't eat anything. Her
head was bald from the chemo. Her skin was gray. She was in
terrible pain. I saw her so vividly in my mind and I got scared
that I would be in her same position soon. So I pretended it
wasn't there and went on with life."*

*Susan's fear led to avoidance, which tragically resulted in
her cancer becoming more advanced. Had she been treated
sooner, she may well have gotten more effective interventions.*

*Letting her fear control her thoughts, emotions, and actions
led to a tragic outcome for her: the cancer had progressed to
a terminal state.*

That is the power of fear.

DISTRESS VERSUS EUSTRESS

In addition to being different driving forces, fear and passion elicit
stress responses that are polar opposites. Later on we'll discuss *eustress*,
the form of stress that can be positive and energizing. But for now let's
talk about distress, the negative aspect of stress. When thoughts and
actions are fear-based, distress is present. To simplify the discussion,
from now on we're going to use the word "stress" to convey just the
negative aspects of stress.

Perfectionism is infused with unwanted emotions. Anxiety, worry,
fear of failure, a sense of vulnerability: all these are types of stress. The
amount of negative energy and stress that perfectionists cope with can
be counterproductive, even harmful. Let's look at the potential impact
stress has on your life.

You're probably pretty familiar with the emotional responses to
stress. When we're feeling stressed out we may be anxious, worried,
depressed, helpless, frustrated, angry, overwhelmed. But fewer people
are aware of the body's physical response to stress: the release of stress
hormones. When we are exposed to these hormones for a prolonged
period of time, just about every system in the body can be negatively
impacted—and the results are not so wonderful.

- *Dermal (Skin):* breakouts, rashes, hair loss, wrinkles

- *Gastrointestinal:* stomach cramps, diarrhea, constipation

- *Immune:* increased susceptibility to illnesses

- *Musculoskeletal:* tight muscles, unexplained pain

- *Cardiovascular:* arteriosclerosis

Another big downside: have you ever noticed that when you're stressed out you can't think as clearly? That's because chronic stress literally shrinks our hippocampus, a part of the brain in charge of certain memory processing. The result? I don't remember. (Just kidding!) No, seriously: high stress levels can reduce our ability to solve problems, focus, concentrate, and feel motivated.

BTP TIP: De-stress to Heal

The power of stress is amazing. There is a field of study called psycho-neuroimmunology that looks at the relationship between psychology (especially in regard to stress) and the neurologic and immune systems. Turns out, stress can cause wounds to heal more slowly and weaken your ability to fight off infections.

And there's more. Stress can even make you fat. Stress hormones can cause increased fat in the abdominal region. Plus, let's face it, when we are stressed out, we do not always make the healthiest food choices. Who reaches for a fresh garden salad when we're worried about taking a big exam or meeting a looming deadline? Many of us go straight to the chips or the cookies—and not just one or two—*lots* of them. Suddenly the whole bag is empty, right?

Stress can also lead to strain in your relationships. I don't know about you, but when I'm feeling overwhelmed, I'm not the kindest, most thoughtful person. In fact, sometimes even I wouldn't want to be around me. I imagine my family feels the same way.

> **BTP TIP: Breathe!**
> One of the fastest ways to reduce stress is to take deep, diaphragmatic breaths. It may seem too simple to be true, but it's not. Deep breathing activates the hypothalamus, which inhibits stress-producing hormones and prompts a relaxation response throughout the body. So next time you notice yourself feeling stress, take five slow, deep belly breaths.

Stress also narrows our perspective. It causes us to focus more on the negative aspects of a situation and minimize the positive ones, even at the risk of deviating from our values and morals. Stress causes us to react in a "survive or die" mentality, which increases the risk we'll deviate from our established rules in an attempt to survive. The problem is that our bodies and minds react as if our stress is life threatening— though most of the time it is not. This negative, "disaster-mentality" focus can cause people to react impulsively or against their true natures. Conversely, stress can also lead to procrastination or avoidance of the situation at hand in an attempt to forestall additional stressful feelings.

REMEMBER THAT STORY I told you in the Introduction: quizzing my daughter for her spelling test while getting ready for a business trip? Well, here's the sad, disheartening place my stressed mind took me that morning:

When I'm thinking rationally, I know that my work is very important. The sense of fulfillment I get from helping others crush their inner critic and create the life they love is incredible! It is my way of helping the world be a better place, even if in just a small way. I truly love what I do, whether I'm coaching the CEO of a Fortune 500 company who'll then apply what we discover to improve his company's work environment (and sales), or helping a stressed out parent dump the mommy guilt.

When my stress levels get high, though, rational thinking can go out the window, and fear can take over. This applies to all of us—even people with a bunch of letters after their names.

If you stuck a microphone in my head during that spelling mishap, this is what you might have heard:

"What kind of a mother flies off to NYC when her daughter is having trouble in school"? (Granted, one misspelled word is not "trouble," but a stressed mind is not a rational one.)

When we are stressed, we may ask ourselves questions, but it doesn't stop there, does it? We also answer those questions. Here were my answers that morning:

"I'm a lousy mother. I should stay home and be here for my children."

Now, when my stress level is low and I'm thinking more logically, I know that I'm not a lousy mother. Although I'm not with my children all the time, when I am home, I try to be present and fully engaged with them. And research supports this quality-over-quantity principle. Plus, I'm not the only supportive adult in their lives; they're surrounded by those who love them.

And yet, with my stress so high, I focused on fear. Fear of being a bad mom. Fear I was ruining their childhood because of my work. Fear that this would have a lasting impact on them for the worse.

Can you relate?

EXERCISE: REFLECTING ON STRESSFUL THINKING

Respond to the following prompts:

Think back to times you were stressed out; describe how your thinking made the situation worse.

_____

_____

_____

_____

_____

Describe a time when you got into an argument with someone over some-thing that, in hindsight, was not that big a deal.

_____

_____

_____

_____

_____

▶

Describe a time when you beat yourself up in your mind.

_____

_____

_____

_____

_____

How do your perfectionistic fears get stronger when you are stressed out?

_____

_____

_____

_____

_____

SO FAR WE'VE been discussing the stress response of fear-based motivation. Its opposite is the stress response of passion-based motivation, which is better characterized eustress. *Eustress* is positive energy that motivates you to *want* to make positive changes. Rather than making you fearful of what might happen, eustress is characterized by resilience, excitement, motivation, inspiration, and enthusiasm. With eustress there is a greater ability to solve problems, think and act in innovative ways, and overcome obstacles—despite any discouragement or cynicism from others. Eustress involves determination, perseverance, and grit.

Examples of eustress include learning something new and interesting, dating someone you really like, building a business you're passionate about, engaging in a challenge that's meaningful to you, watching a scary movie (for some), competing in sports, preparing for an exciting event, developing new skills and talents, and helping others.

Stress or eustress? Your choice. You get to choose which emotions you use to drive every activity in your day. "Really?" I hear you saying. Yes, *really*.

WHERE DOES ALL THIS FEAR COME FROM?

So, where do these fear- or passion-based motivations come from? It's not about what's happening in the "real world" so much as what's happening between your ears. In fact, how you *view* the world actually affects what you *see* in the world.

How you view the world actually affects what you see in the world.

Let's say you're wearing a pair of blue-tinted glasses. Everything looks more blue, right? Now you have a desire for a nice ripe banana. But the only bananas you can find are green. You go from grocery store to grocery store looking for a ripe banana but there are none to be found.

Then you remember you're still wearing those blue-tinted glasses. When you take them off, you see that many of the bananas you were looking at are, in fact, yellow. They are ripe and ready to eat. But when you had those blue glasses on, all the bananas looked green.

We certainly don't go around wearing blue glasses all the time. We do, however, have a lens through which we see the world, and the prescription for that lens is determined by our beliefs. Beliefs are deep-seated thoughts about ourselves, others, and the world. They affect how we think, how we feel, what we do, and even how others interact with us. In essence, our beliefs create our reality.

That may sound a bit too woo-woo to you. Or it may make complete sense.

Here's an example to help illustrate what I mean. Say you're invited to a party where you won't know anyone. It's a rather exclusive event and a lot of influential and interesting people will be attending, but you don't know any of them personally. And, due to the exclusivity of the party, you cannot bring a date.

Let's "try on" two different beliefs to see how each one might affect—or color—your experience.

Our beliefs create a self-fulfilling prophecy.

BELIEF 1: I have to be perfect in order for others to like me. I won't know anyone; I don't even know what to wear. People will judge me. They won't like me.

- *Feelings:* Lonely, nervous, anxious, worried

- *Behaviors:* Fidgeting, tripping over my words, struggling for things to say, standing away from others

- *Others' Reactions:* They avoid me because of the vibe I'm giving off.

- *Thoughts:* "See, no one wants to have anything to do with me. I am a loser. Plus, these people are so stuck-up."

BELIEF 2: Life is an adventure. People are usually kind and want to meet others.

- ◆ *Feelings:* Excited, nervous (in a good way), energized

- ◆ *Behaviors:* Introduce myself to others, ask people questions, be present to what they are saying

- ◆ *Others' Reactions:* They engage in conversation with me, introduce me to their friends, ask me questions.

- ◆ *Thoughts:* "Wow, this event is amazing!"

Do you see how completely different the same event is when viewed from a different perspective?

BTP TIP: Step into Someone Else's Shoes

You get to decide what lenses you wear. Try this: pretend you are a character in a movie who sees the world the way you *wish* you did. Now try to act, speak, stand, and think in the way she would, viewing the world through *her* lens. The more you practice this, the easier it gets.

THE POWER OF THOUGHTS

Our beliefs and thoughts can create our reality. But don't just take my word for it: placebo research powerfully supports this concept. A "placebo" is something that appears to be an active medical treatment but is not. A sugar pill is an example of a placebo.

Placebos have been shown to result in both positive subjective changes (such as self-reported improvements in pain or depression) and positive objective (measurable) reports. Placebo medications, for example, have resulted in brain wave changes similar to those produced by medications given to people with depression, and increased production of dopamine in people with Parkinson's disease. In fact, research shows that the placebo effect can work even when participants are told that what they are taking is, in fact, a placebo. This is a great testament to the power of our thoughts!

One study found placebo effects when relaying information to participants. During a sleep study, participants were randomly assigned to one of two groups. After a night's sleep one group was told they'd slept deeply (as demonstrated by the amount of their Rapid Eye Movement or REM). The other group was told they'd had a light sleep. In fact, these reports were made up. The participants then completed a series of tests to assess cognitive skills. Those who believed they'd had poor sleep scored lower in skills requiring attention and information processing—independent of how much sleep they'd actually experienced.

Our beliefs can become reality.

At a workshop I attended recently, every time someone raised her hand and commented about how a certain concept would affect her life, the instructor would respond: "If you say so."

If someone said, "I could never do that," he'd reply, "If you say so."

If someone else said, "There is no way my wife would agree to that," the instructor came back with, "If you say so."

It got a bit irritating to say the least—until I finally figured out why he said it. This statement was not a flippant phrase, but rather one of wisdom. What you say becomes your reality.

Thoughts Accelerate Stress

What you say to yourself affects how you feel. And how you feel affects what you say to yourself. One feeds off the other.

Imagine that you could stick a microphone in your brain. What would you hear? Your self-talk—your thoughts and beliefs. Now, which kind of thoughts and beliefs do you want running your show: those motivated by fear or those motivated by passion?

Since stress can intensify fear and squash passion, it is important to keep it under control.

In our world today stress often seems ubiquitous—it's just part of being alive. So we're not talking about getting rid of all stress. In fact, some stress can help motivate us to make positive changes. It can provide the eustress we talked about earlier. It is the presence of overwhelming stress, though, that can make things worse and be counterproductive.

EXERCISE: YOUR STRESS LEVELS

Think of stress on a continuum from 0 (no stress at all) to 10 (the most stressed you've ever been). Now, ask yourself:

What is my stress level right now?

_____

What is my average level of stress?

_____

What increases my stress?

_____

_____

▶

What reduces my stress?

_____

_____

What's my stress level when I first wake up?

_____

What's my stress level when I get into bed at night?

_____

When stress levels get to a 7 or higher, rational thinking goes out the window. That's also the level where perfectionist patterns tend to get stronger and stronger.

Your stress level can affect how you view a situation, as the following scenario conveys.

"I was really upset yesterday," said my coaching client, Katy. Her work as a pharmaceutical sales representative has her traveling over a 250-mile-radius meeting with various doctors and their staff.

"Tell me about it," I said.

"I came home after a long day. I drove about a hundred miles to meet with this doctor who basically told me that my product sucks and that he didn't even want some samples. There was ridiculous traffic as I was driving home. I kept thinking about how my manager was going to get on me for not making a single sale that day.

"I get home and my husband, who had promised me he'd be home by five o'clock to let the babysitter go home, was still

not there at seven-fifteen. The babysitter told me he'd called to make sure she could stay later, but he hadn't told me.

"I know he didn't have anything he had to do at work. He was just trying to get a few more things done. I was so mad. He always does this: puts work before the family. I took care of the kids and then took a shower and got in bed. I told him I didn't feel well because I didn't want to even talk to him."

I asked Katy, "What do you think your stress level was, from 0 to 10?"

"A 9," she assessed.

"And why were you so upset?"

"Because he doesn't care about his children or me or the babysitter. He just cares about himself and his work. At least, that's what I was thinking then."

"And what are you thinking now?"

"After I calmed down, I remembered that his boss was in town," Katy said. "And I can see how, given that his boss rarely sees him, going home before five might not look so good."

"What was your stress level when you 'calmed down'?"

"A 5."

"And what is it now?"

"A 3."

"How has your thinking changed from when it was a 9 to now that it's a 3?"

"I realize that I overreacted. I know he loves me and the kids. He was just trying to look good for his boss."

Can you relate?

EXERCISE: THINKING THROUGH STRESS

Think of a time when you were really upset—when your stress level was at least 7 out of 10. Describe what you were saying to yourself at the time.

_____

_____

_____

_____

_____

At some point after this particular incident your stress would have reduced. When it dropped to a 3 or so, what was different about what—and how—you were thinking?

_____

_____

_____

_____

_____

As you can see, we think differently at different levels of stress.

MANAGING STRESS

To better manage stress, we'll want to take a two-faceted approach: proactive and reactive.

Proactive Stress Management

When we manage our stress proactively, we regularly use tools that effectively reduce our stress levels. These could include consistent exercise, meditation, or time with people whose company you enjoy. These also include getting sufficient sleep (seven to nine hours!) and the proper nutrition you need to fuel your body.

Let's talk briefly about these last two items, as they tend to be a source of stress in and of themselves. I *know* that seven to nine hours is a long time. And I get that busy lives call for many waking hours in which to get everything done. As I myself am a mom, wife, head of a household, speaker, writer, psychologist, coach, chauffeur, and occasional cook, well, let's just say that I understand the precious value of time.

Here's the thing: when you get the sleep you need, it's like a whole new life. Research shows that consistently getting a good night's sleep can help you experience:

- ✓ Weight loss

- ✓ Less stress

- ✓ Greater happiness

- ✓ Less illness

- ✓ Improved memory

- ✓ Enhanced performance

- ✓ Boosted creativity

- ✓ Greater energy

- ✓ Even a longer life

So get your Zs!

Food can also have a huge impact on stress levels. Too much sugar or caffeine can increase stress. Processed foods are high in fat, sugar, and salt, which increase levels of the stress hormone cortisol. Dehydration can also stress your body. So choose fresh, whole foods packed with the nutrients we need: protein, good carbs, and healthy fats. (Personally, I start the day with supplements and a nutrition-rich shake. Want to know what I'm using now? Go to www.ElizabethLombardo.com /BetterThanPerfect and I'll tell you.)

BTP TIP: How to Sleep Soundly

One of the best ways to get a good night's sleep is to develop night-time rituals that help you wind down. Screens (TV, iPad, Smartphone) actually excite your nervous system, so shut them down at least thirty minutes before sleep. Dim the lights, read a book, meditate, or take a warm shower to get your mind and body ready to relax and fall asleep.

Reactive Stress Management

Now let's look at reactive ways to manage stress. This strategy is useful when you recognize that your stress level is going up. Whenever you notice your stress is at a 6 or higher, do something helpful to reduce it effectively.

How? There is no one right way. I recommend my clients develop a list of effective strategies that work for them. Why more than one? Because some situations prevent certain actions. For example, if I am onstage speaking to two thousand people and my stress level is really high, I can't ask them to hold on while I go take a bubble bath.

Some approaches my clients use include:

✓ Deep breathing

✓ Meditation

✓ Listening to inspiring music

✓ Going for a walk

✓ Chatting with an upbeat friend

✓ Watching a funny video

✓ Jumping on a bed

✓ Blowing bubbles

✓ Praying

✓ Doing push-ups

✓ Spending some time outside

✓ Doodling

✓ Taking a warm shower

✓ Going for a bike ride

EXERCISE: STRESS REDUCERS

Now it's your turn. Develop your own list of helpful ways to reduce stress—
activities you know will relax you. List at least ten.

1. _____

2. _____

3. _____

4. _____

5. _____

6. _____

7. _____

8. _____

9. _____

10. _____

11. _____

12. _____

Keep this list with you—in your wallet, on your Smartphone, on your desk, in your car. Whenever your stress level is high, do one item on the list. If that doesn't lower your stress level, try another until you succeed.

IT'S ALL GOOD

In my almost two decades of being a clinician, I have worked with some pretty interesting people. Some clients have been homeless, while others had multiple homes. Some had been incarcerated; others had been officers of the law. Some cheated on their spouse, their job, or their government. I've treated people with anger management issues and people who would benefit from yelling out loud once in a while. My clients have included drug dealers and pharmaceutical reps, doctors and very sick patients, people who were obese and people who were so malnourished they had to be tube-fed. Those I've worked with have had diverse backgrounds, cultures, religions, socioeconomic status, and interests. Yet, all these individuals have shared a powerful common denominator—one of the most powerful things I've learned from them: what I now call the Over-Under Principle.

The Over-Under Principle

This principle is an approach to taking a more productive view of behavior (in others) that we consider to be negative. This means that, instead of dwelling on how "bad" the outward behavior is, we remind ourselves that the person's underlying motivation is almost always positive.

Take, for example, someone at work or at school who is bullying others, making negative and condescending comments, even threatening coworkers.

Obviously, bullying behavior is *not* a good thing. But instead of focusing on that fact, let's stop for a moment and consider just *why* bullies bully. Because they are miserable and want to feel better. Their thinking goes something like the following:

- "If I put others down, I will feel better about myself."

- "If I control others, I will feel more powerful."

- "If I make others more miserable than I am, I will be happier—or at least I won't be alone in my misery."

Certainly this rationale is not accurate. And the resulting actions can be extremely destructive. But bullies' underlying motivation—to feel better about themselves—makes sense. I mean, who doesn't want to feel good about themselves?

BTP TIP: Rethink That Hurtful Behavior

Consider how you can use the Under-Over Principle with your loved ones. For example, starting from the premise that you assume your husband means well: when he says something that upsets you, how can you reinterpret what's happening below the surface? Could it be he's having a bad day? That he needs some reassurance? That he wants your attention?

Or when your child does something she knows is wrong, how can you use this principle to better understand why she did what she did? Was she trying to look cool in front of her friends? Or just have some fun?

Using this principle does not excuse what others do. But it does help you better understand where others are coming from, so you can work together moving forward.

Just as the underlying motivation behind behaviors is usually positive, so too is the motivation for "negative" thoughts.

Carly came into my office with a horror-struck look on her face. "I got offered a huge job promotion," she told me.

Not really what I expected.

When I asked her why she looked so worried she replied, "I can't do that job."

"What is the underlying motivation of that thought?" I asked.

"To protect me from screwing up," she replied. "I don't want to fail. I just want to be successful."

"In order to keep that desire to be successful, how might you change your fear to passion instead?"

Carly thought for a bit. "Well, I can focus on my strengths. I can believe in myself. I can ask questions and get extra mentoring if I need it."

"And how would that shift make things different for you?"

"I would be more proactive about getting the assistance and support I wanted, as well as having greater confidence in myself."

"So, how do you feel about the promotion now?" I asked her.

"Excited!"

The Over-Under Principle is key to understanding perfectionism.

FOR A PERFECTIONIST, outward behaviors or self-talk can include:

- Being critical of yourself

- Working excessively

- Procrastinating or avoiding

- Trying to control others

Not necessarily desirable actions, are they? The underlying motivation, though, may include one or more of these positive impulses:

- You want to feel happier and think this approach will help.

- You want to be successful.

- You want others to be impressed by you.

- You want to feel significant.

- You want to help others.

- You want to make an impact.

Certainly all these motivations can be quite positive drivers. The key is to apply these motivators and bring them into play through positive, passionate approaches rather than through ones driven by fear and stress. Don't let your inner critic drive what you do and how you feel.

"We strive for perfection in the areas . . . we can control, and that isn't necessarily what provides contentment and joy for ourselves and, more importantly, for our children."
—Sarah Jessica Parker

THAT'S NOT YOU

Just as perfectionism and the fears that fuel it are not the true you, stress is caused by thoughts inconsistent with the true you. That's why stress doesn't feel good.

Remember the board game Operation? On the "operating table" is the graphic of a man; little metal-edged "sockets" in the table hold various plastic bones of his body. The goal of the game is to remove the bones with metal tweezers without touching a socket's metal edge. If you do hit an edge, the man's nose (a red bulb) lights up and a loud noise announces your clumsy surgical skills.

Now, let's think of the game of Operation as a microcosm of living life. (Hang with me here.) Consider effective play—successful surgery—as being effective living, where everything runs smoothly with no false moves. When we make a wrong move in Operation, the alarm alerts us to the fact that we've deviated from the smooth movements of successful surgery. Similarly, when you have a thought that deviates from the "true you," that lousy feeling you get is just like that alarm you hear when playing Operation. It's simply a feedback mechanism to let you know you're not operating the way you're meant to.

So, when stress occurs—when you have "untrue," defeatist thoughts—do what you would do in the Operation game: simply correct your approach. Make a change, an adjustment, in how you view or interact with the situation, yourself, and others. How? That is exactly what you'll learn in the pages ahead.

USE YOUR FEAR OR STRESS

It can be discouraging to realize just how self-defeating our thinking can be. But rather than beating yourself up for having defeating thoughts, USE them to your advantage. And when I say "USE" I mean:

Unveil your true motivation.

Switch your approach to one of passion and love.

Engage in new behaviors that are more helpful to you.

Let's look at an example of how to use this.

Allie was a client who was stressed about her mother-in-law coming to stay for a long weekend. "She always makes condescending comments about my parenting. It drives me crazy.

"I clean for like a week before she gets here. And I stress out about what to serve because I know she's going to say something about my cooking. I am a nervous wreck."

I asked Allie to really think about what she was saying about her mother-in-law visiting, and then to complete the USE form.

SAMPLE: USE YOUR FEAR OR STRESS

Unveil your true motivation:	I want my mother-in-law to like me and think that her son made a great decision marrying me.
Switch your approach to one of passion and love:	I realize that my mother-in-law needs to feel important and loved. I want her to feel like that.
Engage in new behaviors that are more helpful to you:	Ask my mother-in-law for advice about things she knows, like cooking. Ask her to tell me stories about when my husband was a child.

Switching her approach from fear and anger to passion and love helped Allie feel better about her mother-in-law's visit. It can help you have less stress and more happiness, too. Give it a try.

EXERCISE: USE YOUR FEAR OR STRESS	
Unveil your true motivation:	
Switch your approach to one of passion and love:	
Engage in new behaviors that are more helpful to you:	

> **BTP TIP: Look for the Red Flag**
>
> Instead of getting stressed out about stress, try to think of it as a red flag reminding you to USE it. Rather than being something "bad," stress can be a cue to change your perspective and approach. USE it to your advantage by turning fear into passion.

Now that we've deeply considered what perfectionism is and isn't, its costs and its benefits, and the myriad ways it impacts our relationships with our loved ones, our work, and ourselves, let's learn how we can enjoy a Better Than Perfect life!

PART TWO

7 Strategies to Crush Your Inner Critic and Create a Life You Love

Postmortem Your Past

Evaluate Your Expectations

Reinforce New Roads

Fail Forward

Eliminate Extremes

Create, Don't Compare

Transcend

CHAPTER 5

P: Postmortem Your Past

I F YOU'VE EVER watched *CSI* or any other crime-themed show, you'll be familiar with the concept of a postmortem, a medical examination to determine someone's cause of death. In essence, the medical examiner wants to answer the question, "Why did this happen?"

In this first step of living a Better Than Perfect life, that's what we're going to do too—but with no body parts involved! We want to see if we can determine how your "need" for perfectionism developed. Why do you have these perfectionist patterns that keep getting in your way? When did they start? Yes, it's history, and as much as we'd like to sometimes, we can't change what happened in the past. But there *is* something hugely important that we *can* change. We can reframe how the past continues to affect us in the present and future.

"Stop being who you were and become who you are."
—PAULO COELHO

Take a look at how Jordon Kemper reframed his past to create an even more dynamic present and future.

"I'll never forget when I was a ten-year-old and my travel basketball coach pinched my stomach during practice and commented about my baby fat. It was so embarrassing."

Looking at Jordan now, "fat" is definitely not a word that comes to mind. "Body builder," "athlete," even "model" are all more apt descriptions for this twenty-nine-year-old, whose entire face conveys a broad smile.

I met Jordan through Twitter. His passion and enthusiasm scream off the screen. They are even stronger in person.

Jordan has a mission to help people be healthier. The tagline of his company, OneBody International, is "You only get one. Don't compromise."

Jordan played NCAA college basketball—at least he wanted to. His six-foot-two frame was shorter than others on his team. His coach called him a "Tweener," saying he wasn't small or quick enough to play the shooting guard position, but he also lacked the size to play the forward position. Despite his incredible work ethic and achievements in practice, his coach would not put him in the starting lineup.

"Game after game after game," Jordan told me. "Freshman year. Sophomore year. Junior year. The story never got better, and quitting was a strong option.

"When I was going into my senior season, I thought, 'This is it!' I was voted team captain and knew it was finally my turn."

But it wasn't until a teammate suffered a season-ending injury in the third game that Jordan finally got his first collegiate start.

Jordan's senior season turned out to be one of the best in the school's history. He set several records, including 38 points and 16 rebounds in a single game! In a battle against the number-one ranked school in the country, Jordan poured in 25 points to help his team win.

Jordan started the last twenty-two games of his college career, averaging thirty-four minutes of play per game. And his 8.6 rebounds per game was not only the most on the team, it was the most in the NCAA conference. Not bad for a "tweener." Jordan won many top conference honors following his memorable season.

During those first few years of sitting on the bench waiting for his coach to give him the nod, Jordan had fumed, boiled, stewed, and finally simmered. "I vowed to never allow someone else to determine what I could and couldn't do," he said. "I promised myself I would be successful without a boss or company dictating my moves."

So Jordan was intrigued when his friend Dr. Steve Hryszczuk told him about USANA Health Sciences, an independent business opportunity where he could improve the health of others.

"Teaching people to be healthier and be my own boss? Are you kidding me? This was the perfect fit for me."

Jordan started with less than a thousand dollars in his bank account. Six years later, his business crossed the million-dollar mark. USANA nutritional products are an integral part of his OneBody International business.

Sitting on that bench all those years, Jordan developed some perfectionist traits. Now with his business, hungry to see his associates succeed, Jordan often struggles with delegating responsibilities when his "control-freak tendencies" kick in. Early on, his I-can-do-it-better-myself attitude slowed down the growth of his team.

At first, allowing others to be creative, lead conference calls, and even speak at public events was very challenging for Jordan. He knew that if he just took over the task himself, results would be immediate, high quality, and comfortable. This was a frustrating time.

It was only when he learned to hold back his perfection-istic, controlling tendencies that his organization really took off. "When I stepped back to let my leaders lead," he recalled, "the growth was explosive." He realized that others on the team have incredible ideas, methods, and suggestions different from his own. That is the beauty of a team.

Jordan believes wholeheartedly that we all should be thankful for the painful trigger moments in our lives. That coach in middle school who pinched his stomach became the impetus behind Jordan working out consistently thereafter. "Since that day, I've been committed to exercise." From the pain and embarrassment also sprouted massive awareness and sensitivity to people dealing with overweight concerns.

Today, Jordan often appears onstage, electrifying capacity crowds with figures like Dr. Oz and Darren Hardy. Jordan says he thanks God for the painful moments, because they left beautiful scars.

"Turn your wounds into wisdom."
—OPRAH WINFREY

THE BIRTH OF "THE NEED TO SUCCEED"

Can you relate to Jordan?

Did something ever happen in the past that you vowed *never* would happen again?

Do you ever feel that if you aren't doing everything perfectly, everything will fall apart?

Doing a postmortem of your past is a vital first step in the Better Than Perfect program because it will provide clarity about *why* you do what you do. I'm certainly a big proponent of focusing on the present and future when working with my clients. At the same time, I've also found it helpful to uncover the *origin* of the issue, because addressing the cause can be like healing a deep wound. Unless you explore where your perfectionism sprang from, just adding new skills might be only a quick fix—like slapping on a Band-Aid—that may or may not help with the healing.

Make the past a present to your future by doing a postmortem.

> **BTP TIP: Why Revisit Your Past?**
> True, you can't change the past, but we are not trying to. We are trying to change how the past continues to affect you. Here's what we often miss. The past is not what continues to hurt us. It's our interpretation—what we "learned," what we took from the past—that still affects us. The event is over. Our thinking is what keeps it hurting us.

My clients often tell me, "I know that some of my perfectionism doesn't really make sense, but I just can't get rid of it." Rationally, they are aware that some changes would be helpful, but their hearts are telling them, "Don't you dare!"

Can you relate?

Underlying this attitude is usually a deep-seated belief developed at some point in life, whether long ago or recently, a belief that says, "I cannot screw up!" To try to find the root cause behind this crippling mind-set, let's look at three ways in which perfectionism can originate:

- Modeling

- Rewards

- Avoiding Punishment

MODELING

There is an old tale about a woman making Thanksgiving dinner. She attacks the turkey with her cleaver, cutting the turkey in half prior to putting it into the oven. No easy task. Her daughter, watching her mother struggle, asks, "Why do you do that?"

Pausing for a moment and looking at her daughter, the woman thoughtfully responds, "I don't actually know. It is just something my mother always did. Let's call Grandma and find out."

While on the phone, Grandma explains, "We used to have an oven that was too small for the turkeys I would buy. So, I had to cut them in order to fit the entire thing in."

The woman could see her own oven easily housed an entire turkey. But, for years, she had given her blood, sweat, and tears to cutting her turkeys in half. By adopting what her mother did as "law," she had been wasting her time and energy. How aggravating!

Can you relate to this story in terms of how you developed your perfectionist patterns? What did you see others do in the past that may have led to your perfectionism?

+ Did you see your mother or father constantly working?

+ Did a parent often work late hours or on weekends?

+ Did one or both bring work home?

+ Did you develop the belief that "work is more important than fun"?

+ Did you have a parent who was exceptionally neat and believed "I must keep the house clean all the time in case someone comes to visit"?

IN A HOLIDAY season *Washington Post* article titled "For Women, It's the Most Stressful Time of the Year," Brigid Schulte poignantly wrote about women who have long-standing holiday rituals, like baking dozens of cookies or decorating every crevice of the house. Why? Because that's what their mothers did. Of course, their moms may not have also worked a full-time job and had children enrolled in 7.2 extracurricular activities . . .

Or maybe what was modeled for you was the opposite of perfectionism. For example, one client explained that her father was always late and never did what he said he would do, especially chores around the house. His behavior and attitude upset her mother so much she eventually divorced him. Based on this early experience, my client formed the belief that, in order to be loved in a marriage, she would need to do the opposite of what her dad had done. As a result, she developed perfectionistic rules for both herself and her husband.

How about you? As a child, did you hear messages such as:

◆ "I hate to be late—it is a sign of disrespect."

◆ "A real man works hard and takes care of his family's needs."

◆ "Work defines who you are. Do a lousy job at work and you are out."

EXERCISE: REFLECTING ON MODELED PERFECTIONISM

Think over the messages you assimilated from watching your parents or other influential people in your life.

Who demonstrated perfectionistic qualities?

_____

_____

_____

_____

Who was the opposite of "perfect"?

_____

_____

_____

_____

What did you take away from how these people acted?

_____

_____

_____

_____

REWARDS

Let's face it: you probably wouldn't have become a perfectionist unless you'd gotten rewards of some kind as a result of your actions. Here's how my perfectionist patterns began when I was an adolescent:

Lunchtime was the worst. No one to stroll to the cafeteria with and complain about how much homework the teacher had assigned. No one to look for as I carried my tray to a table. No one to laugh with as we ate.

Right before the summer of seventh grade, my family moved to a new state, which meant a new neighborhood and leaving my old friends behind. My parents enrolled me in a small all-girls school that went from grades one through twelve. Entering in the seventh grade, I was one of just a few new students; most of the other girls had known each other for years. I was the outsider. And it felt lousy.

I wanted to have friends. Even more, I wanted to feel good about myself and feel worthy. But I didn't.

While some might have thrown themselves into sports or other activities, I chose to fixate on academics. Studying became my focus in life. I studied during lunch when I sat by myself. I studied on the school bus when, in retrospect, I might have spent that time making friends. I studied when I got home, going above and beyond anything my teachers expected. I even studied on the weekends. I'd memorize every single word in my notes, to the point where I could re-create twenty, thirty, even forty pages of notes practically verbatim, without looking.

The emotional truth is I studied as if my life depended on it. In my mind, it did! Somehow, I had developed a mentality that told me, "If I get A's then I'm okay. If I get A's then people will like me. If I get anything less than an A, then I'm worthless."

As time went on, I made friends and became much more social. My "need" to get perfect grades stuck with me, though. While I may have looked successful to those around me, I was dealing with an almost-addiction that got in the way of living my life fully. I would decline invitations to important events (including a friend's wedding when I was in graduate school that promised to be a blast) because I "had" to study. In retrospect, I see that I would have been just as successful academically had I taken part in regular activities and events outside of my schoolwork.

Seventh grade was when my pattern of perfectionism started. And, as time went on, it began to rear its head in other areas of my life.

Remember the Over-Under Principle—that there's almost always a positive motivation behind most outward behavior, even when the behavior is not so positive. My own perfectionism developed from the desire to feel good about myself by getting good grades. When I moved to a new school in the seventh grade, I went from getting B's, C's, and D's to getting A's. Why? While moving was out of my control, I could control one part of my life: studying. And I appreciated being rewarded by teachers and my parents for getting those top grades. My entire sense of self got wrapped up in trying to get perfect marks.

Here's another example:

"I was an Army brat," Ben told me. That meant Ben and his family frequently moved during his childhood. "My dad was a sergeant. We lived in six different places before my seventeenth birthday.

"It was hard growing up constantly moving. You had to keep proving yourself over and over.

"The only time my dad and I really interacted was when it came to sports. We used to shoot hoops sometimes together. And the more I practiced, the more he would make comments to other people about me: 'You should see my son's hook shot.' I loved that attention from him."

Ben took steps to get more and more of that positive attention from his father—and other kids. He spent hours every day practicing his dribbling, shooting baskets, getting others to play a pickup game.

"Every evening before I went home, I used to make myself get fifty baskets in a row. If I got up to forty-nine and missed one, I would make myself start all over again. It had to be fifty. It had to be perfect."

It is human to want to be accepted and liked by others. As they strive to achieve that attention, though, perfectionists often develop an assumption about their conduct based on these early events. "People are proud of me because of my success" becomes generalized to "People will be proud of me *only* if I am successful." As a result, the need for success develops and stays. And stays.

EXERCISE: REFLECTING ON PERFECTIONIST BEHAVIORS

Can you relate to being rewarded for what you did and then thinking, "I need to do it like that again . . . every time"?

Think back to when you were younger. Jot down some early experiences in your life when you were rewarded for your perfectionist behaviors.

_____

_____

_____

_____

_____

AVOIDING PUNISHMENT

Were you criticized when you were younger for not excelling?

Did you get in trouble for anything less than 100 on your tests?

Did you get ridiculed for a mistake and vow never to make it again?

That's what happened to Jordan, whom we met at the beginning of the chapter. Here's another example:

> *In 2009, pop star Kesha had an unpaid cameo on Flo Rida's number-one hit "Right Round." By November 2013, she was jubilantly performing onstage with Pitbull at the American Music Awards, singing their number-one hit "Timber." Two months later, Kesha sought residential treatment for an eating disorder.*
>
> *The year before, in an interview with* Seventeen *magazine, she said, "I remember every person who told me I couldn't do something or that I was ugly or too fat. People in the music*

business were like, 'You're never going to make it.' I see them now and I'm like, 'Ha!'"

In her pursuit to "make it," Kesha signed with a well-known producer and manager who reportedly pressured her about her weight.

According to her mother, "One time on a conference call, Kesha's manager was screaming, 'You need to lose weight! I don't care what you do . . . take drugs, not eat, stick your finger down your throat!' She was doing everything and not getting thin fast enough, and that's when she first became bulimic."

Approximately one out of every fifty American women suffers from bulimia, which is characterized by eating large quantities of food and then purging, frequently by self-induced vomiting.

Oftentimes the bingeing is stress-related. The purging is usually an attempt to gain some control over the amount of calories that were just consumed. People with bulimia and other binge-eating disorders often struggle with perfectionism, too, feeling guilt and shame for their lack of "perfect" eating.

What about you? Can you relate to Kesha? Have you taken steps to try to avoid punishment or negative consequences, such as ridicule from others? How has this contributed to your perfectionism?

BTP TIP: Show Me the Money!

Research has found that people can be more motivated to prevent loss than to acquire gains. For example, in one study, the members of one group were offered a bonus at the end of the year if they reached certain achievements. Members of the other group were given that bonus money up front and told that if they did not reach a certain level of achievement, they would have to give it back. The result? The second group had significantly better results.

EXERCISE: REFLECTING ON PUNISHMENTS FOR IMPERFECTION

Describe times when you were criticized, made fun of, or punished for not being perfect.

_____

_____

_____

_____

_____

_____

_____

_____

_____

_____

_____

_____

ACTION STEPS: CONDUCT YOUR POSTMORTEM

Step 1: Identify Your Origin Story

Step 2: Arrive at Your A-ha

Step 3: Identify Your Triggers

As President John F. Kennedy once said, "Our problems are man-made, therefore they may be solved by man [or woman]." And in order to fix a problem, it helps to understand what caused it.

If you haven't yet done a postmortem on what initiated your perfectionist tendencies, I encourage you to do one right now. That pivotal experience or circumstance—and the message you took away from it—is still a driving force in your life on a daily basis. Unfortunately, this is also preventing you from thriving. Follow these Action Steps to perform a postmortem. Then we can use that information to help you transform your life.

Step 1: Identify Your Origin Story

While reading this chapter, you may have started to develop some ideas about where your perfectionist traits came from. Maybe you can remember a specific event when you vowed never to make a certain mistake again. Perhaps you recall times when you received praise or attention for doing something "perfectly." Maybe you can see how perfectionism was modeled for you in someone who was influential in your life.

It's time to write down your story. You may have already zeroed in on a pivotal event or circumstance that sparked your perfectionism, and that's a great first step. Now we're going to focus on putting the details of that experience on paper.

In my practice, clients are often resistant to writing out these events and details. "I know what I'm thinking. This seems like a waste of time," someone will tell me. In reality, it's vitally important to actually write down your story rather than just think about it. Why? There are thousands of thoughts swirling around in your head at any moment—some you are aware of and others you're not. And, because those *thoughts are in your head*, it's all too easy to view them as facts rather than interpretations.

When you take these recollections out of your head and put them on paper, you can see them in a different way. Information that you once accepted can be analyzed to see how accurate and helpful it really is. Remember, it doesn't have to be perfect. This is not a writing contest or English class where the quality of your writing (or even the spelling) matters. Just write whatever comes to mind.

EXERCISE: REFLECTING ON THE ORIGINS OF PERFECTIONISM

Describe a single event or multiple events that prompted you to develop your "need" to be perfect. Don't hold back.

What was the incident?

_____

_____

_____

_____

▶

Who was there?

_____

What did they say and do?

_____

_____

What did they not say and not do?

_____

_____

What did you say, think, and do?

_____

_____

When did you hear someone use the phrase "should" or "should have"?

_____

_____

What was the take-home message for you?

_____

If you're having difficulty identifying a specific time, then simply write whatever comes to mind when you reflect upon the following questions.

Who in my past has demonstrated any type of perfectionist qualities, such as:

- All-or-nothing thinking

_____

- Incessantly working

_____

▶

- Focus on work over fun

_____

- The need to have things neat and/or clean

_____

Also ask yourself:

When was I rewarded in the past for "successes" that came from any perfectionistic tendencies?

_____

_____

What were times in my past when I felt embarrassed about being wrong or messing something up?

_____

_____

BTP TIP: Journaling

Journaling, or writing out your thoughts and feelings, can have a positive impact on your life. James Pennebaker, PhD, who has spent decades researching the benefits of written emotional disclosure, has found that writing out your deepest emotions and thoughts can result in improved health (including fewer doctor visits and stronger immune function), greater resilience to stress, increased grade point average, and improved mood.

The bonus? No one else has to read what you wrote. It can be for your eyes only. Give journaling a try.

Step 2: Arrive at Your A-ha

Sometimes when people try to overcome their perfectionism they stop after identifying the events or situations that led to their perfectionism. In my experience, this is a huge mistake. Simply reliving the past is like pressing on a bruise. It hurts and hinders healing.

This is why the next step is so vital: it allows you to *learn* from the past. When you let it, the past serves a purpose. Now it's time to discover what that purpose may be.

Simply reliving the past is like pressing on a bruise. It hurts and hinders healing.

Let's find your a-ha. That's a pivotal moment when you go from confusion to clarity, from distress to discovery, from victimization to verification.

Think of your favorite thing to do when you were young. Maybe it was playing with a doll, a toy, or a game. (Personally, my favorite thing to do was dance around and sing songs from *Grease*, but that is another story . . .)

Now ask yourself, "Is that still my favorite activity?" Most likely, the answer is "Are you crazy?" As you've grown up, your childhood interests have stopped serving you. Just as you (probably) don't play with your old toys anymore, you may also want to toss out some of your childhood beliefs. Many of them don't serve you anymore, so why hold on to them? The same can be said for other outdated thoughts you may have developed about perfectionism.

Without realizing it, you may be letting your life be limited by beliefs that you developed as a child or that you globalized from one specific event. By doing this, you've placed a ceiling on yourself that constrains the impact you can have in this world. Your perfectionism puts a damper on the joy and fulfillment you could be experiencing. It silences and inhibits the true you. It also affects the people around you—and not in a good way.

BTP TIP: Let It Go

If you continue to find yourself hurt by an event that happened twenty years ago, or have negative behavior patterns that have persisted over the years, now is the time to realize you *can* change these unproductive patterns. It is not the event but *your thoughts* about the event that continue to affect you. Follow the steps in this book to help free yourself from the past.

EXERCISE: EXAMINING YOUR ORIGIN STORY

Answer these questions:

What was the message I took from the experience(s) I wrote about above?

_____

_____

What fears did I develop?

_____

_____

What assumptions did I make about how I thought I needed to act?

_____

_____

Understanding both why you developed your perfectionist rules and their uselessness to you today is essential to becoming Better Than Perfect.

"I was never good enough for him," Tim said about his father.

Tim's looks could have gotten him on the cover of Esquire, *especially his piercing blue eyes, and his bank account could have landed him on the front page of* Forbes. *By most accounts, he was a wildly successful, self-made man. He was the president of his own business, to which he devoted the majority of his time and energy.*

Tim's wife insisted that he see me because, according to her, "He works all the time. He makes enough money but never thinks it's enough. He'll say he's coming home at six o'clock and won't show up until after eight."

Tim explained, "I have full intentions of leaving when I say I will, but then I think 'I'll respond to just one more email,' and suddenly it's two hours later."

He shared with me his fear of not having enough money. "I know it may sound crazy to other people, but I'm afraid of losing it all. I feel like I need more and more before I can feel satisfied."

Actually, it did not sound crazy. It was something I hear over and over from even extremely wealthy clients. They develop a sense of financial perfectionism, continually striving for more money and assets. It can be incredibly stressful for the individual, as well as for family and coworkers.

Growing up in a two-bedroom apartment with his parents and three siblings, Tim recalled, "Dad was the disciplinarian. If you did something wrong—anything wrong—he was the one whose wrath you would face. He was a stickler for grades. Anything other than an A, and you would hear about it. A D would get you the belt; sometimes so would a C if he was in a bad mood."

"Why do you think he did that?" I asked him.

"He was a mean son of a bitch," Tim quickly replied.

I kept quiet for a bit as Tim sat in silence, deeply exploring my question.

"He had a really tough childhood," Tim eventually resumed. "Had to drop out of school when he was in tenth grade to get a job to help support his family. They were dirt poor.

"His entire life it has been tough for him to find work. He never wanted us [Tim and his siblings] to have to go through the stress he'd gone through. He wanted us to go to college and have a better life than he ever did."

Tim paused and then added, "He was scared to death we would turn out like he did."

Tim's father wanted a better life for his children. Being motivated by fear, he expressed this desire aggressively rather than in a loving and inspiring way. And Tim interpreted this experience as a need to be perfect financially for his own family.

The a-ha's Tim realized were:

- I was scared of being berated by my father.

- I decided if I were perfect, he would not yell or get out the belt.

- Really, I wanted my dad's acceptance and love.

- I realize now that my dad *did* love me, in his own way.

- He never really experienced love as a child and didn't know how to show it in a healthy way.

- I also realize that what is important is believing in myself.

- When I believe in myself, I can love myself and more fully love others, including my wife and kids.

- I can work hard to provide for my family and at the same time enjoy my family and life.

Now it's your turn.

EXERCISE: IDENTIFYING YOUR A-HA'S

What a-ha's can you glean from your postmortem?

_____

_____

How can you apply those realizations to your life?

_____

_____

Use your past to your advantage.

Step 3: Identify Your Triggers

Triggers are experiences that tend to initiate or perpetuate perfectionistic traits, pushing us into the perfectionism zone. For example, whenever Tim was with his father or even thinking about his father, he tended to work more hours, checking and rechecking his work. This response could be triggered even by smells associated with his dad. "Sometimes when I smell cigarettes, I get tense and go back to that little boy who just wanted his dad to love him."

Both increased stress and feeling out of control are common triggers. One journalist client told me, "I realize that when I'm really stressed, it takes me forever to finish an article because I keep going over and over it. When I'm not feeling so overwhelmed, though, I'm better at knowing when it's ready to be sent out."

How about you?

EXERCISE: IDENTIFYING YOUR TRIGGERS

Now, identify a time after the initial event you discussed above when your perfectionism reared its head again.

What were you doing?

_____

_____

Who was with you?

_____

_____

▶

What were you saying to yourself?

_____

_____

Describe any sensory triggers, such as smells, sounds, or sights.

_____

What emotions tend to trigger your perfectionistic tendencies?

_____

_____

What patterns do you notice?

_____

_____

Now use your discoveries to help yourself. Determine what you can do *instead* of thinking and acting in perfectionistic ways when those triggers show up.

For example, when I am feeling stress, I tend to revert back to perfectionist patterns. (I also do what I never thought in the world was possible: I forget to eat. The hunger makes me even more stressed and irritable, which just boosts my perfectionist pattern.) The following guidelines help me in stressful moments by reminding me of more effective responses to stress.

SAMPLE: EFFECTIVE RESPONSES TO PERFECTIONIST TRIGGERS

TRIGGER	CURRENT RESPONSE	HEALTHIER CHOICE
Busy schedule	Increased stress	Meditate and exercise (even if for shorter periods than is ideal)
Upcoming presentation	Trouble sleeping	Schedule sleep, establish wind-down routine to relax before sleeping
Traveling	Forget to eat	Schedule meals (including putting a reminder on my Smartphone)

EXERCISE: EFFECTIVE RESPONSES TO PERFECTIONIST TRIGGERS

How about you? Plan in advance for the moments when your perfectionist tendencies are most likely to be triggered. Figure out the best strategies to override them now, when you're calm and not being influenced by them.

TRIGGER	CURRENT RESPONSE	HEALTHIER CHOICE

▶

TRIGGER	CURRENT RESPONSE	HEALTHIER CHOICE

CHAPTER 6

E: Evaluate Your Expectations

A s CHILDREN WE all had expectations for ourselves, didn't we? (Personally, I imagined myself being a doctor or an Avon Lady.) As adults we still have expectations; they're just (usually) different from those of our childhoods.

Expectations are strong beliefs about the future—what we anticipate will occur. They differ from goals in that a goal is something you strive to achieve, while an expectation is something you predict *will* take place. If the expected outcome does not transpire, disappointment often results. In my clinical practice I've found that rigid expectations can be the essence of unhappiness.

"All I ever wanted to do was be a pilot."

Steve was sitting in my office, slouched over in a wingback chair. He looked older than his fifty-two years.

Referred by his primary care doctor, Steve was struggling with depression. It quickly became evident that depression was not new to him.

"From the time I can remember, I always knew I was supposed to be a pilot. All through childhood I dreamt about flying, I pretended to fly everywhere. I spent countless hours putting together toy planes.

"At the age of nine, I had my whole life planned. I would go to college with an ROTC scholarship, go into the Navy when I graduated, and become a Navy pilot, just like my dad had been.

"All that ended when I turned eighteen. I was having my eyes checked as part of a routine checkup for college and learned I was color-blind. I have something called protanopia, which means I can't really see the difference between reds and oranges and yellows. I'd had no idea. With this realization, I knew my life was ruined."

Those who are color-blind are prohibited from becoming a pilot. "My dreams were squashed. I felt like I had practically died.

"I had no idea what to do. Finally, my parents suggested I go into accounting. I was always pretty good at math— thought I would need it when I was a pilot. So I went into accounting and became a CPA. Sure, it provided a pretty good living (Steve was a VP in his company), but I never actually enjoyed it. I always felt like my life ended the day I learned I was color-blind."

Steve married and had two children. He loved his family but could not escape his deep disappointment in himself for not being a pilot.

Then one day Steve learned his job was being eliminated. "I felt almost like when I first learned I couldn't be a pilot. After devoting twenty years of my life to them, they just dumped me. They should have done something to keep me. They owed that to me after all that I gave them."

That happened eighteen months before I started seeing Steve. Since then, his mood had prevented him from seeking further employment. He had plummeted into a state of depression that was debilitating—for him and those around him. His wife threatened divorce if he didn't get a job. The bill collectors called daily. One of his children had to drop out of college because they could not afford the tuition.

Steve's unfulfilled expectations of becoming a pilot when he was younger had clouded the rest of his life. His expectations of how a company should treat its employees further damaged his sense of well-being.

How about you?

Did you ever have a dream that was crushed, perhaps related to work, sports, a relationship—something you wanted badly?

Did you ever feel let down or even destroyed when what you expected did not happen?

Have unfulfilled expectations ever been a source of guilt, shame, anger, helplessness, hopelessness, or even worthlessness?

In this chapter we'll explore how expectations can lead to true discontent, distress, and even destitution. We will also outline how to excel without expectations while still maintaining the desire to make positive changes.

There is a key distinction that we need to make here. There is nothing wrong with striving to make things the best they can be. It is the reaction that perfectionists have when they fall short of their perfectionist goals and expectations that we want to explore and challenge.

IF . . . THEN . . .

Perfectionists like orderly progressions: "If I do X, then I get Y." For this reason, many people (myself included) liked the predictability of school. "If I study and memorize this information, then I will ace the test." And usually their predictions about school and grades became reality.

There are many other contexts in which we see the "If . . . then . . ." mentality.

- *Health:* "If I work out five times each week, then I should lose weight."

- *Happiness:* "If I achieve this goal, then I should be happy."

- *Relationships:* "If I keep dating, then I should find the one."

- *Work:* "If I work hard, then I should get promoted."

- *Fun:* "If I keep my arms straight and rotate my body, then I should hit the golf ball straight down the fairway."

Can you relate to any of these examples? What happens when your expectations don't play out?

WE'VE ALL HAD things that we really wanted in our lives that haven't materialized. Perhaps you wanted to become a doctor, make a million dollars before age thirty, or get married (again). We've also had people disappoint us because they did not live up to our expectations. Rationally we know that life doesn't always progress the way we expect. And that can be disappointing. But for a perfectionist, deviations from expectations can be overwhelming.

> *"I feel like a complete failure," Shannon told me. It was a Tuesday morning, our second session together. The sun was shining through the windows, lighting up the right side of her face and body.*
>
> *Shannon was a forty-one-year-old who, at least by society's standards, was extremely successful. Climbing the corporate ladder, she had broken through many proverbial glass ceilings. She made excellent money—by almost anyone's standards. "I worked hard for all of this," she told me. "I never got anything handed to me. I knew from a young age that I had to work hard to win."*
>
> *Shannon was sitting in my navy blue chair with tears welling up in her eyes, talking about her difficulties getting pregnant.*
>
> *This is an issue more and more people seek my help for. In fact, according to the CDC (Centers for Disease Control and Prevention), about 10 percent of women ages fifteen to forty-four have trouble conceiving or staying pregnant. This statistic only increases with age.*

"I spent my entire adult life trying not to get pregnant," Shannon confided. *"Now it's all I want."*

There was an overwhelming sense of helplessness in her voice. *"It's just so hard. I've done everything—I mean every-thing—the doctors have told me to do: hormones, injections, acupuncture. Tom changed his entire work schedule for five months to make sure we could do our homework assign-ments. I changed my eating, I tried meditation, I've tried it all. And it's not happening!"*

For Shannon, the stress of not being able to conceive was heightened by her expectations: *if you follow the doctor's orders, then you will have a baby.* When what she expected didn't occur, she felt even more helpless and hopeless. Not only did this cause emotional trauma for her, it also put a huge strain on her marriage and her effectiveness at work.

Can you relate?

EXERCISE: WRITE YOUR OWN "IF . . . THEN . . ." EXPECTATIONS

If I . . .

_____

then . . .

_____

▶

If my spouse . . .

_____

then . . .

_____

If a coworker . . .

_____

then . . .

_____

If my friend . . .

_____

then . . .

_____

IT'S NOT JUST ABOUT YOU

Perfectionism affects more than the perfectionist. It can significantly affect the lives of the people you love. Nowhere do I see this more vividly than when it comes to the perfectionistic expectations held by parents, like these below.

- "My child is taking Mandarin, Spanish, and French. She can count to ten in four different languages, and she's only four years old."

- "We do flashcards with my three-year-old every night."

- "My seven-year-old Suzie is taking ballet, hip-hop, soccer, photography, painting, horseback riding, and Latin after school this semester."

Parents want their children to succeed, and certainly there's nothing wrong with that. It's when that desire translates into pushing children excessively that problems can arise, because stress caused by perfectionism in the parents can take a heavy toll on their children. I often see the impact on kids' emotional health (six-year-olds who cry when they get one problem wrong on their math test) and their physical health (exhausted thirteen-year-olds who consistently stay up late to get all their extracurricular work done).

BTP TIP: Let Kids Fail

As a society we are focused on helping our children feel good about themselves—a positive motivation, to be sure. Sadly, we often do so to the detriment of their well-being. When we let our children "fail," they learn how to deal with not getting an expected outcome and, equally important, how to problem-solve to eventually achieve what they want. So, keep your children physically safe *and* let them fail. It will help them develop grit, resolve, resilience, confidence, and courage.

IN HIS BOOK *How Children Succeed: Grit, Curiosity, and the Hidden Power of Character*, Paul Tough shares research findings on what truly predicts success for our children. It turns out that being able to do multiplication tables at the age of six is not one of them. Resilience, perseverance, the desire to learn, optimism, and self-control are predictors of success—immediate and future.

The takeaway? Yes, keep helping your children learn their school-work. And also help them develop qualities such as optimism, resilience, curiosity, and perseverance. Let them play, let them imagine, let them be passionate about a subject matter or activity. And let them mess up—often—so they can learn that (1) you can still have a good outcome when your expectations don't come to pass; (2) failing doesn't mean you need to stop; and (3) you can learn from past mistakes. Essentially: failing doesn't make you a failure. (We discuss this more in Chapter 8: "Fail Forward.")

It isn't just excessively pushing one's children that can be problematic; perfectionistic parents can go in the opposite direction as well, discouraging their kids from even trying to achieve a big, ambitious goal.

"My son wants to be a lawyer," said the hairdresser as she was assessing her work. "I keep telling him there's no way he could ever do that. I mean, how am I going to pay for college, much less law school?"

Jessica had an expectation about her son: he could never be a lawyer because they could not afford the tuition. In trying to protect him from getting his hopes up needlessly, Jessica had instead crushed his dream.

"My heroes are the ones who survived doing it wrong, who made mistakes, but recovered from them."
—BONO

FEELING ENTITLED

Another way expectations can show up is through entitlement. That's when you believe you have the right to certain privileges or benefits. We've all heard about diva celebrities, for example, who insist on specific types of bottled water and only green M&M's in their dressing rooms. But entitlement is an issue for more than just the superstars. I frequently see a sense of entitlement crop up, especially with the Millennial generation.

"She's driving me crazy!"

Doug, a fifty-seven-year-old executive, was not talking about his wife, but about a twenty-seven-year-old employee named Amber.

"She questions everything I say and do. She balks at working late, informing me she has a CrossFit class to go to. And she constantly expects me to tell her what a great job she's doing, even if she is just doing her job. She also thinks she can tell me what to do when it comes to implementing our plan. Hello, I am the boss here!"

One booming area of my consulting business focuses on helping different generations work together optimally. Relieving the tension between them requires an understanding of different interests and approaches. Emotional intelligence is key.

"The other day she asked me when she could expect her next promotion. Her next promotion? She just got promoted last year. She hasn't done anything to warrant a promotion. Who does she think she is?"

The Millennial generation, defined as those born in the 1980s and 1990s, has an outlook that differs from that of Doug's generation. Millennials tend to value learning, mentorship, creativity, and figuring things out. They do not work to live but rather live to work—they want to find purpose in what they do. They like working as a team and do not believe in a hierarchical system. They expect to be treated as an equal and to be appreciated on a regular basis.

They also love their technology.

Doug continued, "She and the younger staff come into a meeting and immediately put their cell phones on the table. Sure, the ringers are off, but it's so disrespectful. They are constantly glancing down at their phones, typing in a message, and chuckling as they read whatever pops up on their screens. I just want to throw them on the floor and smash them."

Despite Doug's frustration with what he saw as Amber's sense of entitlement, he could not deny that she worked hard. She had also on more than one occasion come up with out-of-the-box thinking that had improved the productivity of their team.

Before getting upset about other people's sense of entitlement, it's important to understand where these views may be coming from. Entitlement often comes with expectations: "because of this, I should get that."

Much of that mind-set is a by-product of both upbringing and the messages absorbed in childhood, as we discussed in Chapter 5: "Postmortem Your Past." Doug's story continues.

As part of my executive coaching with Doug, I was able to spend some time with Amber. "So, Amber," I asked, "how would you describe your working relationship with Doug?"

"Overall I think it's good. He gets so upset, though, when I ask him any questions. Doesn't he know I am just trying to understand why he asks me to do what he asks me to do?

"He got really upset when I asked him for a promotion. I was pissed off about that. I've been working really hard and doing a good job. I deserve a promotion. Don't tell him, but I am looking elsewhere and starting to get my résumé out."

The Millennial generation is used to getting trophies for basically showing up. They're used to situations where everyone on the team receives a medal. Given this, it makes sense that they feel entitled in other areas of their lives. (Of course, just because it makes sense, I'm not saying it's helpful!)

So, essentially, Amber's sense of entitlement—that she deserved another promotion—was so strong she chose to seek employment elsewhere, despite the fact that she had a good salary, enjoyed her work, liked her team members, and felt appreciated overall.

A sense of entitlement puts you on the fast track to unhappiness. When you don't receive what you think you're entitled to, disappointment, anger, shame, and sadness can result.

BTP TIP: Working with "Those Kids"

If men are from Mars and women are from Venus, Boomers are from Saturn and Millennials are from Jupiter. Each generation has its own way of seeing the world. The key to interacting productively is learning each other's language. Here are some tips on how best to work with Millennials. (Keep in mind that each person is unique, regardless of the general characteristics of his or her generation.)

* *Provide leadership and guidance.* Millennials want mentorship; they love to learn and develop.

* *Focus on purpose.* Provide meaning for *why* they are doing something. Millennials resist performing a task just "because that's the way it's done." They want to understand the reasoning behind the action. When they do understand, they're more motivated to follow the plan.

* *Encourage their self-assurance and can-do attitude.* By negating those attributes, you run the risk of alienating them. Instead, use these traits to get Millennials to optimize their work.

* *Be flexible.* And be open to feedback yourself.

If I had asked Amber to chart why she decided to start sending out résumés, it might have looked like the table below.

SAMPLE: "I DESERVE X BECAUSE . . ."

I DESERVE . . .	BECAUSE . . .	WHEN IT DIDN'T HAPPEN, I . . .
a promotion.	I have been doing my job well.	felt underappreciated and decided to look for a new job.

EXERCISE: "I DESERVE X BECAUSE . . ."

Create a chart for yourself as well. Write out a few times when you thought, "I deserve X because of Y" but did not get it. How did you feel? What did you do?

I DESERVE . . .	BECAUSE . . .	WHEN IT DIDN'T HAPPEN, I . . .

Rationally, we know that life does not always happen the way we'd like it to. Life did not read the textbook of life, so it doesn't always pan out in a logical or orderly fashion. But knowing this rationally doesn't always help us emotionally.

Life did not read the textbook of life.

WHOSE RULEBOOK?

Deeper than predictions of what will happen, a perfectionist's expectations tend to be rooted in her rulebook. We all have certain rules about how we think life *should* be—for example, how a loving spouse, caring friend, or successful person *should* act. These rules influence how we view ourselves and others, how we feel, how we react, and even how we perceive the world.

> *I was being interviewed for a news program in New York City. The male interviewer asked, "Why do women have a rulebook?"*
>
> *I responded, "We all have a rulebook—men and women. It's just that men's rulebook is more of a pamphlet and women's is more like a manifesto."*

In our minds, these expectations are not just rules; they are more like facts. These beliefs are so strong that we often forget they are *perceptions* rather than truths. To us, they are inflexible and set in stone. But despite how much impact these rules have in our lives, we often don't even realize they exist. That is, until a rule is broken.

Nina had been divorced for four years and was just getting into what she had thought might become a serious relationship. But then things took a turn for the worse. At least Nina thought so.

She was brokenhearted because her boyfriend didn't seem to be as interested in her as she had hoped. "He went out with his guy friends twice in the past three weeks. Obviously I am not that important."

What?

Nina had a rule—a belief—that men who go out with their guy friends don't want to spend time with their girl- friends. In essence, in her mind a man who loves a woman wants to be only with her—all of the time. Even during foot- ball season.

Once Nina verbalized this rule, we explored how accurate and, equally as important, how helpful it actually was.

Nina realized it was not working for her. Sure, if he never wanted to hang out with her, that might indicate he's not that into her. But wanting to be with his friends was understand- able—and maybe even a good thing.

So, instead of getting upset the next time Dave wanted to go watch the game with his pals, she encouraged it. "Sounds like fun. Have a great time," she replied genuinely.

Dave's response? He gave her a huge hug and asked her out to dinner the following evening.

Nina had never realized the stringent rule she had created about dating. When Dave broke this rule, though, she found herself needlessly upset and heartbroken.

THE POWER OF SHOULD

Another way to identify the rules we create for ourselves and others is the use of the word "should."

The other day I was walking out of my house when I smelled something pungently putrid. I had noticed a bit of an unpleasant odor earlier, but had assumed it was the trash can in the garage. I soon learned that wasn't the source.

Playing hound dog, I started sniffing the area, trying to find the odorous culprit. I went into different rooms in my house, stuck my head in closets, and went downstairs. Finally, I realized the overwhelming stench was coming from the top of the refrigerator in the basement, where a package of raviolis had been mistakenly left out. And, boy, did they stink up the place!

"I was raised to sense what someone wanted me to be and [then] be that kind of person. It took me a long time not to judge myself through someone else's eyes."
—SALLY FIELD

Like those rotten raviolis, the word "should" may be unassuming, but it is extremely powerful and pungent. *Should* is also problematic in that it goes beyond mere predictions—it also includes a heavy component of judgment. When we think someone *should* do something, we are passing judgment.

When we *should* ourselves, we feel guilty or shameful. We view ourselves as less than, not good enough, maybe even worthless. And these judgments feel lousy. When we *should* someone else, we experience anger and resentment toward that person. In our mind, he or she messed up *big* time (even if it was really a relatively small event in the grand scheme of life).

Remember charades? That's the game where one team member acts out cues without speaking in order to get the team to identify a certain word, phrase, or title. Well, if I were to do a charade of the word "should," it would be a big finger wagging in front of your face—or someone else's. A *should* feels like that judgmental finger wagging back and forth.

BTP TIP: De-Should Yourself

A seemingly harmless word such as "should" really can be quite destructive. And it's more than "just semantics." The judgment surrounding *should* basically says, "You're just not good enough." And even if you don't rationally believe it, your subconscious will accept it as real. Follow the exercises in this chapter and de-should yourself; you'll notice the benefits in your emotional and physical well-being, relationships, and even work. Why? Because in addition to our emotions, *shoulds* affect our behaviors.

If, for example, you decide, "My husband should walk Petunia tonight since I took her out this afternoon," but then he doesn't spontaneously jump up and grab the leash at the usual hour, you might get upset, with thoughts like "Are you seriously not going to take the dog out tonight?!" perhaps echoing in your head. Let's say you then leash the dog yourself, muttering passive-aggressive comments under your breath like "Must be nice to have a servant."

"You can be happy, or you can be right. If you want to be part of a couple and win every argument, you're in trouble."
—Steve Harvey

Regardless of the specifics in any situation, *should* does nothing but create tension and disharmony with others.

Can you relate to being upset at someone for what you thought he or she *should* have done? We'll learn more about how to optimally deal with this in the Action Steps below.

For now, ask yourself, "How often do I use the word 'should'?"

Then, for the next three days, pay close attention to every time you hear the S-word, whether it comes out of your mouth or someone else's. You may be surprised at just how often it happens, as did my client Carl, who told me:

"I could not believe how many times I say it. And how many times everyone says it. I started calling out my girlfriend on it every time she said it."

I'm not suggesting you start "playing shrink" with your loved ones (that may *really* drive them crazy!). I am asking you to be more aware of how you and others freely throw around this judgmental word. Then take it one step further. Whenever you hear the word "should" come out of your mouth, stop and ask yourself what rule this *should* is declaring. One client imagined a giant finger wagging every time she said the word. The image made her laugh, allowing her to take a step back to assess her rules more objectively.

RULES FOR OTHERS

Let's look more closely at rules for others we may have developed over the years. What comes to mind when you read these sentences?

EXERCISE: IDENTIFYING YOUR *SHOULDS*

A true friend should . . .

_____

A loving spouse should . . .

_____

Good people should . . .

_____

In-laws should . . .

_____

Strangers should . . .

_____

Salespeople should . . .

_____

Politicians should . . .

_____

Did any of your responses surprise you?

The set of rules you've created is influenced by a wide variety of factors, including your culture, your childhood, your parents' rules, your friends' rules, the media's rules, and experiences in the past (even as recently as earlier today). Our rules tend to be so ingrained in our subconscious that we often don't even realize we've adopted them. They seem like facts rather than the subjective regulations they actually are. When I ask new clients about their rules, they usually have no idea what I am talking about.

Why do we have these rules about how others should behave?

Again, the Over-Under Principle is in play. Our motivation is most likely positive: we want to be able to know how to interpret others' actions and words. If someone doesn't like us—or thinks we are wonderful—we want to, understandably, know that. By having "rules," we can more easily decipher how someone else views us.

The problem is not the motivation for these rigid expectations, but rather their consequences. When we react to one of *our* rules getting broken as if it were a *true* rule—that is, one that everyone knows and agrees with—we are basing our reaction on inaccurate information.

Consider this scenario. As the CFO of a company, your job is to report on its financial health and develop plans for the following year. What if you based all your reports on inaccurate numbers—numbers that did not represent the true profits or losses? How well would you be able to function as CFO? Not very well, right?

And yet, when we emotionally and behaviorally react as if our own made-up rules are truths, we are basically doing the same thing. This not only causes unnecessary stress for ourselves and those around us, but also results in our doing and saying things that aren't true.

A friend of mine was visibly upset with me. When I asked what was going on she responded, "You never called me back."

"I am so sorry," I said. "I never got any message from you. When did you leave it?"

"I didn't leave a message. I called your cell phone three times. You must have seen my missed calls, but you never reached out to me. What kind of a friend is that?"

Seriously?

Then I started thinking about her rulebook. And, rather than get upset at what I initially saw as a ridiculous reaction, I decided to focus on empathy.

"I'm sorry. I now realize that a missed call from you is an indication you want to talk. I have to admit, I get tons of calls every day and don't really pay attention to the missed calls, just the messages. From now on, can you please leave me a voicemail when you want to chat or, even better, just send me a text? I care a lot about our friendship and want to stay connected."

I chose not to force my rules upon her, or even explain why I may have thought she was unjustified in her distress. Taking this approach helped threefold: (1) I felt less annoyed; (2) my friend felt loved; and (3) it made it possible to figure out how to communicate going forward.

RULES FOR YOURSELF

Even more than creating rules for others, a perfectionist has a ton of rules for herself. See which of these ring true for you.

- *"I should be more successful."*
- *"I should be in better shape."*
- *"I should help out my neighbors."*
- *"I should have known that."*
- *"I should get more sleep."*
- *"I should always look presentable."*
- *"I should get more done during the day."*
- *"I should cook dinner for my family."*
- *"I should have a cleaner house."*
- *"I should be more grateful."*
- *"I should be happier."*

How often do you apply the word "should" to yourself? How do you feel when you don't achieve the result you expected: shame, guilt, helplessness, hopelessness, worthlessness?

Rules can help make sense of the world. If left unchecked, though, they can create obstacles.

THE EMOTIONAL COST

Consider a time when you hoped for something that didn't happen, anticipated an event that did not occur, or predicted an outcome that never took place.

Which emotions did you feel?

+ Anger

+ Fear

+ Frustration

+ Guilt

+ Helplessness

+ Hopelessness

+ Resentment

+ Sadness

+ Shame

+ Worthlessness

What did you do with these feelings?

+ Acted in angry or passive-aggressive ways

+ Withdrew from others

+ Stopped trying

+ Gave up

+ Vowed never to let it happen again

+ Overate or engaged in an unhealthy activity

When their rules are broken, perfectionists tend to react strongly—and persistently. They are prone to depressive episodes, angry outbursts, and emotional meltdowns.

Why is so much emotion tied in to expectations? There are a few reasons. First, expectations help a perfectionist to make sense of what could happen in the future—and to have some sense of control in the often senseless and unpredictable world. If you *think* that doing X will result in Y, and then it happens that way, it feels good. There is safety and comfort in knowing what will happen.

For perfectionists, unpredictability can be interpreted as being out of control. (This is another example of all-or-nothing thinking.) And experiencing a lack of control can feel scary. This is called learned helplessness, a term that refers to feeling powerless—the sense that there is nothing you can do to make things better. In essence, you feel as if you have no control over what's happening. Learned helplessness can lead to greater stress, a depressed mood, and giving up. It's why the cable guy who doesn't show up as scheduled drives you batty. It's also a key factor in why airline customers yell at ticket agents even though they know the agents aren't responsible for the canceled or delayed flight.

A perfectionist's disappointed expectations can also trigger intense emotions because of the tendency to overpersonalize. This means a perfectionist uses her expectations to help her determine her worth. To a perfectionist's mind, not getting hired by her dream company has nothing to do with the company's skill requirements or team chemistry; it's clearly because the perfectionist wasn't good enough. Or, as with Nina above, her boyfriend wanting to spend time with his guy friends had nothing to do with the boyfriend or male bonding or even football: it was instead about his not loving her.

Essentially, the power of expectations for perfectionists goes well beyond the expectations of nonperfectionists.

PERSONALIZING OTHERS' REACTIONS

The holiday season—late November through the beginning of the New Year—offers a great opportunity to explore expectations. Each year, I am inundated with media interviews and coaching requests on "how to get through the holidays." The way I see it, holiday stress is provoked by a sense of perfectionism.

Any of these sound familiar?

- "I should get her the perfect gift."

- "I should prepare a delicious meal."

- "We should be more grateful."

- "My mother should be more supportive."

- "My family should all get along."

Why might you think these *shoulds*? If you really delve into them, all these statements are rules that contribute to how you feel about yourself. For example, what happens if you don't buy a friend "the perfect gift"?

When I asked a client this, she responded, "Then she will question how well I know her. I mean, if I got her something she hated [notice the all-or-nothing thinking here], *she would have to wonder if I really know her."*

"What kind of friend gets her friend something she'd hate?" I asked.

"A terrible friend."

"And what kind of people are terrible friends?" I asked.

"Losers."

To my client, not giving the perfect gift translated into being a loser. Ouch.

"When you judge another, you do not define them; you define yourself."

—WAYNE DYER

Can you relate?

Perfectionists tend to be extremely judgmental. They are quick to judge those who don't meet their standards—themselves included. In fact, it is their strict self-judgment that brings them to judge others.

Think about it: if you're consistently criticizing yourself, then you're also going to be critical of others; critical thoughts would just be your natural form of thinking. As best-selling author Wayne Dyer said, "When you judge another, you do not define them; you define yourself."

ACTION STEPS: CHANGE YOUR RULES

Step 1: *Identify Your Rulebook*

Step 2: *Put Down the Gavel*

Step 3: *Take Control in New Ways*

So, what's in your rulebook? As I've said, most of us are not even aware we have a rulebook, much less know its rules. In the process of determining what's in your book, just remember: it's not a matter of rules being "right" or "wrong." Let's try to remove any sense of judgment and simply determine how accurate and helpful these rules are. We want all of our thoughts to be as accurate and helpful as possible, don't we?

Step 1: Identify Your Rulebook

Complete the statements below. Answer with the first thing that comes to mind. Don't filter or judge what you're thinking. Just write it down for now.

EXERCISE: INDENTIFYING YOUR RULEBOOK

When I am sad, a good friend should . . .

_____

_____

_____

After I have had a long day, my partner should . . .

_____

_____

_____

It is okay to relax when . . .

_____

_____

_____

▶

To show love, a parent should . . .

_____

_____

_____

To feel good about yourself, you need to have . . .

_____

_____

_____

If a parent is doing her job, the child should . . .

_____

_____

_____

I should . . .

_____

_____

_____

I should never . . .

_____

_____

_____

It is okay to play when . . .

_____

_____

_____

▶

To succeed, you should . . .

_____

_____

_____

People show respect by . . .

_____

_____

_____

If I do what I should, then . . .

_____

_____

_____

Do any of your responses surprise you?

Now examine each one, and ask yourself the following questions:

- How accurate *is* this rule?

- How flexible is this rule?

- How helpful is this rule? What are the consequences?

- How can I change the rule to make it a more accurate and helpful guideline?

For example, here is what Doug, the baby-boomer business executive earlier in this chapter, had to say about employees attending to their phones during a meeting:

SAMPLE: IDENTIFYING YOUR RULEBOOK

MY RULE IS . . .	HOW ACCURATE, HELPFUL, OR FLEXIBLE IS THIS RULE?	MY NEW AND IMPROVED GUIDELINE IS . . .
If someone brings out his phone, it's a sign of disrespect. People should know to put their phones away—in their offices, for instance.	It makes me furious because I think that it's a slap in the face. In reality, I get that this is just a part of life for the younger generation.	I choose not to personalize how other people use technology. At the same time, I'm also going to be more assertive. Instead of expecting them to know how much their phones bother me, I am going to make all conferences phone-free zones.

Now you try. Complete the following table.

EXERCISE: IDENTIFYING YOUR RULEBOOK

MY OLD RULE IS...	HOW ACCURATE, HELPFUL, OR FLEXIBLE IS THIS RULE?	MY NEW AND IMPROVED GUIDELINE IS...

Step 2: Put Down the Gavel

What would your life be like if you stopped judging yourself and others so much? For many, this concept seems foreign, even impossible. As one client said to me, "Judging helps me know right from wrong. If I didn't judge, how would I know how to act?"

There is a difference between discernment and judgment. *Discernment* refers to being able to see things clearly, including what is different or similar about situations. *Judgment* takes this one step further by identifying something as good or bad.

One way to reduce judgment is to simply get rid of that one (stinky) word: "should." Try replacing the word "should" with "would like to" or "it would be great/good/ideal if" and see how it feels.

Consider the following:

SAMPLE: TRANSFORMING "SHOULD" INTO "WOULD LIKE TO"

"SHOULD" STATEMENT	CONSEQUENCES	"WOULD LIKE TO" STATEMENT	CONSEQUENCES
I should get that promotion.	◆ Feel stressed ◆ Push myself at all costs ◆ Step over others in order to get ahead ◆ Act entitled ◆ Speak to my boss about it ◆ Feel anger and shame if I don't get it	I would like to get that promotion.	◆ Work hard ◆ Tell my boss I'm interested in the position ◆ Ask for feedback on increasing the likelihood I'd get the promotion ◆ If I don't get the job, though disappointed, I'll get feedback and take steps to keep improving

Simply replacing the word "should" with a more benign phrase immediately takes the judgmental pressure off yourself. Removing that increased stress frees up energy you can instead use to determine how to accomplish your goal.

Now you try. Once you identify a "should" statement you recently made or that you tend to use frequently, complete the following table.

EXERCISE: TRANSFORMING "SHOULD" INTO "WOULD LIKE TO"

"SHOULD" STATEMENT	CONSEQUENCES	"WOULD LIKE TO" STATEMENT	CONSEQUENCES

> **BTP TIP: Stop the "Musterbation"**
>
> I think of the words "must" and "ought" as cousins to the word "should." Just as *Saturday Night Live*'s Stuart Smalley might say, "Don't *should* all over yourself," in the field of cognitive behavioral therapy we sometimes say, "Stop the *musterbation*."

Step 3: Take Control in New Ways

When your expectations or even just your hopes don't come to fruition, it's easy to feel powerless. But it's important to realize that, while you cannot always control what happens, you always have at least some control.

In the field of psychology we differentiate between problem-focused coping and emotion-focused coping. With **problem-focused coping** we work to tangibly improve a problematic situation. With **emotion-focused coping** we instead work to improve our emotional reaction to a problematic situation. Let's look at an example to explore the difference between the two.

One of the biggest stressors for employees in the business world is corporate downsizing. A company's announcement of pending restructuring often results in uncertainty and a sense of helplessness. I'm frequently approached by HR departments seeking help for the plummeting morale and work performance associated with company restructuring.

Potential job loss can create emotional turmoil for anyone. When employees learn change is on the horizon, helplessness can take over. Why? Because most of us aren't familiar with emotion-focused coping, where we ask ourselves: "What can I do to feel better about this situation?" Not knowing this option, many of us default to feeling help-less, as if "there's nothing I can do to make this situation better." When that happens, we're less able to employ problem-solving coping, where we work to tangibly adapt to the situation at hand.

At one company in transition, I gave a workshop where I asked group members to identify ways they could cope by using both prob-lem-focused and emotion-focused approaches. Here's what they came up with.

SAMPLE: PROBLEM-FOCUSED AND EMOTION-FOCUSED COPING

PROBLEM-FOCUSED COPING	EMOTION-FOCUSED COPING
Talk to management	Take steps to reduce my stress
Get résumé together	Focus on helping others and making a positive contribution applying my strengths and values
Start calling friends at similar compa-nies and ask about any open positions	Remember to take breaks to re-energize
Volunteer for a task force	Focus on my gratitude that I still have a job

While both problem-focused coping and emotion-focused coping can be beneficial, we often neglect emotion-focused coping. This is vital because, as discussed in Chapter 4: "Fear Versus Passion," feeling overwhelmed by stress prevents us from thinking or functioning as cre-atively or effectively as we might. And creative, effective functioning could be what wins the day.

> **BTP TIP: How to Get Control**
> Whenever you feel you have no control over what's happening around you, remind yourself: *I always have choices.*

EXERCISE: PROBLEM-FOCUSED AND EMOTION-FOCUSED COPING

Now you try. Think about a time when you felt you had no control—perhaps over something related to work, a relationship, or your health. Then think about both problem-focused and emotion-focused approaches that could have helped you better handle the situation. As you come up with ideas, keep in mind that the purpose of this exercise is not to judge or criticize what you actually did, but simply to help you see other options that might aid you in the future.

Describe the situation.

_____

_____

_____

_____

_____

_____

_____

PROBLEM-FOCUSED COPING	EMOTION-FOCUSED COPING

So, the next time you encounter a situation where you feel as if you have no control, remember there are always options. Step back, take a deep breath, and look for ways you can apply both problem- and emotion-focused coping strategies to help you navigate the situation at hand.

While we don't always have a say in what happens to us, we always have choices about how we react—though oftentimes we don't realize it. For example, I remember one afternoon conducting a training at the nonprofit Dress for Success, an international organization dedicated to promoting "the economic independence of disadvantaged women by providing professional attire, a network of support, and the career development tools to help women thrive in work and in life."

Various participants shared their stories. Joan told us about her journey from using crack cocaine and living on the street to coming to Dress for Success and trying to get a job to support her family.

When I asked how she felt about turning her life around, she looked at me as if I was speaking a different language. "I didn't have a choice," she responded.

Yes, she did have a choice; she could have stayed in the street. But something in her decided she needed to make enormous, difficult changes. Recognizing the significance of that accomplishment made her feel empowered and proud of all she was doing to change her life. Joan was a great example of living a Better Than Perfect life.

CHAPTER 7

R: Reinforce New Roads

Many people with perfectionist traits have strong thoughts and beliefs that direct and dictate their lives. There's that old rulebook again! Despite how intense and powerful these ideas are, they are often automatic and habitual rather than deliberately formulated—even to the extent that we're often not even aware we have them. We are, however, able to see their repercussions. And, sadly, they are not always the consequences we want.

"I don't know what I am supposed to do."

Caroline was referring to her life purpose. And, though her attire and hair looked perfectly in place, I soon learned she didn't feel truly put together.

Her three children were growing up. One was in college, the other two in high school. Now that the middle child had a car and drove the younger one to her activities, there were no more carpooling duties for Caroline.

Twenty years earlier she had said good-bye to the business world, where she had been climbing the corporate ladder. For the next two decades she had devoted her time and energy— her life—to addressing the needs of her family. Now, she felt, they didn't really need her anymore.

Caroline was experiencing what often happens when roles change: a loss of self-identity. For the past twenty years, Caroline defined herself as a "mother"—an involved and engaged mother. Up until that point she'd experienced meaning in her life by taking care of her kids.

Now, questions such as "Who am I?" echoed through Caroline's head. "I feel like I'm nobody. I have no purpose. No one needs me. What am I supposed to do?"

I see this loss of self-identity often: in parents whose children get out of diapers and into school, or when the kids go to college; when someone loses a job or retires; when a relationship ends; or when an illness disrupts a person's capabilities. Essentially, the way these people have been defining themselves is no longer applicable.

Can you relate?

Do you ever question your purpose in life?

Do you ever feel lost, not knowing which path to take?

Do you have any self-defining thoughts that no longer serve you?

The really good news is that you get to decide how you view yourself and your life. You get to choose your perspective, your meaning, and your passion. Caroline did it. Let's see how you can do the same.

OPEN-FIELD THINKING

Imagine standing before an open field. The waist-high yellow-green grass billows in a light breeze. You want to get to the other side, but find no established route through it. How do you cross?

Because there is no beaten pathway, you can choose to forge whatever path you want. It could be a straight path, a squiggly path, or a complete loop.

Let's say you decide to go cross the field along a diagonal path. As you proceed, your feet press down the grass, leaving a trampled path.

The next time you want to cross the same field, how will you do it? You'll probably take the path you established—the path of least resistance.

If you keep walking that same path over and over again, it will get so worn there'll be no more grass, just dirt. And each time you cross the field, you'll most likely take that same path, right? Doing so continues to forge a deeper path into the dirt.

Our thinking is very much like this field.

A belief is a well-worn pathway deeply rooted in the field of our minds.

When we have a thought, certain nerves fire in a pathway to create that thought. Once we've created that thought pathway, we're more likely to have that thought again and again. In essence, that neural pathway becomes the more frequently taken path—the one of least resistance. And eventually it will become automatic. I refer to this process as Open-Field Thinking (OFT).

A belief is a well-worn pathway deeply rooted in the field of our minds.

There is a purpose to these pathways: they make information easier to process. At any given moment, you are exposed to billions of bits of information. Because you cannot possibly process that much data at once (some of us have enough trouble processing just one bit at a time!), these pathways help us navigate our world more efficiently.

"The difficulty lies not so much in developing new ideas as in escaping from old ones."
—John Maynard Keynes

One of the ways the brain helps us traverse our world is by creating schemas. In psychology, the term "schema" refers to a person's set pathway or preconceived ideas about something. Think of schema as a type of label we put on ourselves or others.

Here's an example of what I mean. We start to develop schemas in our childhood. We see a four-legged animal next door and Mom tells us it's a "dog."

On a walk in the park, we come across another four-legged creature. This one is much smaller than the one next door, and has different-colored fur. "Dog," we say. "Yes," Mom replies with a big smile.

We are developing a schema of what a dog is.

When we're in the car, we drive past a farm with four-legged animals. "Dog," we say, pointing at the creatures. "No, honey, those are horses."

This feedback—that a horse is not a dog, that more than one type of creature has four legs—helps us refine the schema of *dog* so that, eventually, even if we encounter a dog breed we've never seen before, we can still differentiate between a dog and a horse—or any other four-legged creature.

Schemas are integral to our thinking because they are shortcuts to processing information. And the more efficiently the brain can process multiple stimuli—like a farm of four-legged animals—the more sophisticated stimuli the brain is able to process—like various types of bulldogs.

While this has benefits, on the other hand, schema can also perpetuate stereotypes and deep-seated beliefs, many of which may not be all that helpful. This can make it difficult to absorb new information that doesn't match the schema—like trying to push a square peg into a round hole, not seeing that the two, though similar, are indeed different.

"If someone is going down the wrong road, he doesn't need motivation to speed him up. What he needs is education to turn him around."
—JIM ROHN

If we think of this in terms of the OFT concept, schemas are well-forged pathways—like a deep rut in our dirt path—that make it difficult to create a new pathway.

Now let's consider schemas in relation to perfectionism. An example of a schema held by many perfectionists is "If I am not perfect, then I am 'damaged goods.'" Such people view themselves as internally flawed—never good enough. These beliefs make the perfectionist feel incapable, inferior, deficient, even worthless. Some spend all their energy trying to prove their worth. Others' sense of unworthiness is so deep they don't let people get close to them, for fear of their inadequacies being discovered. As you can imagine, it can be difficult to break free from such strong beliefs.

FORGING NEW PATHS

Now, what if we want to have a new thought? That new thought would represent taking a different route through that grassy field. This time, rather than the diagonal path, let's say you choose to walk in a loop instead. When you forge this new route, what happens to the grass? The grass crushes under your feet, and much of that grass stays down. If you looked back you could see your new pathway etched into the field.

Now, the next time you want to cross this field, which path do you take?

> *"If you don't like the road you're walking, start paving another one."*
> —DOLLY PARTON

Forging a new neural path is as easy as simply choosing to beat a new route through your grassy field. The thing is, a once-trodden path is not the well-trodden one; while you can see the grass squashed down on the new path, the old path—with its grass worn down to dirt—is still the path of least resistance. Although we do not *have* to, we tend to take the path of least resistance. And when we take that path often enough, we "choose" it without thinking. That well-worn path, that repeated thought, becomes more automatic. During this process the "choice" moves from our conscious mind—where we're really aware of it—to our subconscious mind—where we're not aware of it at all.

Put simply, your conscious mind includes what you are aware of: the thoughts you consciously say to yourself. And while we do have brain chatter, there's only so much we can consciously process at one time. So our brains developed shortcuts to allow us to navigate a complicated environment. As a result, we often don't even realize we're having all the thoughts we have; if we did, we'd get overloaded.

Conversely, your subconscious stores and retains a vast quantity of information—the words to a song you haven't heard in years, what the kitchen you had growing up looked like—including the deep-seated beliefs you've cultivated for your whole life, from your childhood all the way to the present. And though we'd like to think it's our conscious selves manning our ship, in fact it's the subconscious that's predominantly in control. As well as having a huge impact on our conscious minds, our subconscious commands much of our bodies, emotions, and behavior.

In his best-selling book *The Ant and the Elephant: Leadership for the Self*, my friend and speaking coach Vince Poscente makes a very revealing comparison. He cites the research findings of Lee Pulos, PhD, who determined that, in every second, the conscious mind uses two thousand neurons. In comparison, within that same second the subconscious uses *four billion* neurons. The ratio between the two is similar to the difference between an ant (the conscious) and an elephant (the subconscious).

Think of a game of tug-of-war. The conscious mind, represented by the ant, holds one end of the rope, and the subconscious mind, the elephant, holds the other end. Guess who's going to win pretty much every time? The elephantine subconscious.

THE ELEPHANT VERSUS THE ANT

This great disparity is why just telling yourself something new doesn't allow you to convert your belief in one go. Even repeated new statements, such as those used in affirmations, often don't work on their own. Why? That ant may struggle for all he's worth, but he's still up against an elephant.

For example, I had a client named Becky, who had worked with another therapist before me. Becky came in saying, "I want to be happy, but I feel like a failure. My other therapist told me to just repeat, 'I am a success' over and over. It didn't work. Actually, I feel like even more of a failure now."

Repeating affirmations like this can make you feel inauthentic. Though you're saying one thing, on a deeper level your subconscious refutes that statement.

Let's consider Becky's experience in terms of Open-Field Thinking. Her established pathway is her deep-seated belief: "I am a failure." Even though she one day started to forge a new pathway (an affirmation: "I am a success"), her subconscious kept taking the old pathway—the path of least resistance.

Or, on slightly different terms, imagine you're not just walking your worn path through the field—you're pushing a wagon along that path. You've crossed this way so often the wheels have forged deep ruts in the dirt path. Now, if one day you decide to consciously push the wagon out of the rut and onto higher ground, you can succeed— but as soon as you stop this conscious effort the wagon slips back into its rut, its well-worn subconscious path.

Similarly, you can consciously forge a new thought, even more than once, even repeatedly for a while, but that doesn't stop your sub-conscious from slipping back onto the old path, without your even realizing it.

So let's take stock for a moment. We've taken the time to reflect on our lives, and we've decided to make a change. But we're up against some tough obstacles, with the heavyweight complex functioning of our neural paths working against us at every turn. Is it hopeless? No! Fortunately, one of the means by which we strengthen unhelpful behaviors can be instead used to our advantage. Read on.

Frequent and repeated use isn't the only means of forging a path-way; emotion also has the power to deeply imprint a path. A thought occurring at the same time as an emotion will make a deeper imprint on the brain than the same thought experienced without emotion. And the more intense the emotion, the stronger the thought will be. Strong emotion is like carrying a three-hundred-pound weight as you cross the field on your established path. Your heavier weight will forge even deeper tracks.

So, emotion has the power to forge deeper paths. Unfortunately, research shows that our brains tend toward a negative bias. Negative information is more readily noticed, attended to, and stored. Why? Simply put, for our own protection. If our ancestors, hearing a suspi-cious rustle of a saber-toothed tiger in the bushes, had thought, "I'm sure it's nothing," they wouldn't be ancestors. For tens of thousands of years, humans attending to negative thoughts was literally a matter of life and death. Thus, negative information is more "sticky," which is why that negative chatter in your mind can hang around so persistently.

So how do we make changes in our beliefs? New information, such as an affirmation, enters your mind via the conscious brain. It may stay at that outer layer temporarily or be absorbed into the subconscious. For new information to enter the subconscious, we need extensive repetition *coupled with* emotion. We'll talk more about how to make positive changes more lasting in the Action Steps section.

"You create your own universe as you go along."
—WINSTON CHURCHILL

THE INTERNAL GLASS CEILING

We've all heard about the proverbial glass ceiling that prevents women and others perceived as minorities from advancing up the career ladder. Equally as important, I believe, is the *internal* glass ceiling.

The restrictions you put on yourself create your internal glass ceiling, which may or may not concern your gender, ethnicity, or background. An internal glass ceiling is the product of critical thoughts and beliefs, such as "I can't do that" and "That's beyond my reach."

BTP TIP: If You Picture It, It Will Come

In an interview published in the July 2012 issue of *Self* magazine, Fergie of The Black Eyed Peas talks about the power of visualization. Visualization is based on changing your subconscious to benefit you. Fergie visualized getting a Grammy Award, which she, along with her hip-hop group, eventually achieved—eight times!

It was while reading Sheryl Sandberg's *New York Times* best-selling book, *Lean In: Women, Work, and the Will to Lead*, that I truly realized the power of our internal glass ceiling. Sandberg, the chief operating officer of Facebook, encourages women to step up to leadership positions at work. She talks about the need for changes in both external policies and the internal dialogue in women's minds. It is this internal dialogue that I call the internal glass ceiling.

Sandberg cites a 2008 Hewlett-Packard study that found that, while men will apply for a job as long as they meet 60 percent of the position's criteria, women won't apply unless they meet 100 percent of the criteria. That's a powerful internal glass ceiling. Can you hear the all-or-nothing thinking there?

Sandberg writes, "Women need to shift from thinking, 'I'm not ready to do that' to thinking, 'I want to do that—and I'll learn by doing it.'"

What internal barriers have you erected in both your professional and personal lives?

If you stuck a microphone in your brain, what would you hear yourself saying about your limitations? Do any of the following sound familiar to you?

- ◆ "I can't do that because . . ."

- ◆ "I would love to do this but can't."

- ◆ "It is not fair that I can never . . ."

- ◆ "No matter how much I want it, that will never happen."

- ◆ "Maybe in another lifetime, but not in this one."

"No one can make you feel inferior without your consent."

—ELEANOR ROOSEVELT

With perfectionism comes a desire to engage in only the activities that yield desirable results. It's not that we're afraid of hard work—perfectionists are notoriously hard workers. It's that we're desperately afraid of failing.

One study found that fifth graders who were told they did well because they worked hard were more likely to continue to do so—and to continue to succeed, even with more challenging tasks. In contrast, the students who'd been told they did well because they are smart were less likely to persevere, attributing undesired results to lack of ability, and were less likely to take on more challenging tasks.

We'll discuss this more in the next chapter. Until then, consider for a moment: what would your life be like if you removed these self-imposed perfectionistic limitations?

> *"When you're passionate about something, you want it to be all it can be. But in the endgame of life, I fundamentally believe the key to happiness is letting go of that idea of perfection."*
> —DEBRA MESSING

THE ROADS OF YOUR PAST AND FUTURE

Perfectionists tend to be ruminators. Just as a cow chews her cud again and again, so do many perfectionists chew on their thoughts, sometimes ad nauseam. This happens when we dwell on the past ("I shouldn't have done that") or continually worry about the future ("What will I do if . . . ?").

With regard to dwelling on the past, it's often difficult for perfectionists to let go, to accept what's already happened. For example:

* "I should have said . . ."

* "He instead should have . . ."

* "If only ____ had happened . . ."

In wishing an outcome had been different from what actually occurred, it's as if we're attempting to change history. But reliving events or berating ourselves or others over what can't be changed does no one any good. Certainly it's important to learn from the past—as we discussed in Chapter 5: "Postmortem Your Past." It's also important to accept, rather than resist, that which has already happened.

BTP TIP: Be Present

Instead of being upset about the past or worrying about the future, be present. That means be mindful of what is happening in the here and now. Work to quiet the negative chatter in your mind. Focus on what's taking place around you and within you. Experience what is happening at this very moment. Mindfulness is a powerful tool that can help us feel less stressed and more happy.

With regard to worrying about the future, perfectionists have a lot of practice. If you were to suggest to a perfectionist that he stop worrying, he might look as if you'd proposed he stop brushing his teeth. Why? As a client in the middle of a divorce told me, "Worrying helps me prepare for what may happen."

In reality, though, worrying can stress you unnecessarily. Let's look at a metaphor I often share with my clients.

When I opened my first private practice, I lived in Dallas. Being a big fan of warm weather (I keep my thermostat at home set at 78 degrees), I loved how warm Texas was in the fall, winter, and spring. The summers, though, were *really* steamy, sometimes 100 degrees for weeks at a time. As soon as you set foot outside air-conditioned spaces, it was tough to keep your cool.

On the other hand, the winters do get cold (at least by my definition). There are times each year when the temperature drops below freezing.

Let's say you stopped by my office in Dallas in the middle of August. It's 101 degrees out, and you're happy to be in my air-conditioned waiting room. When I come out to greet you, I'm wearing a winter coat, ski hat, mittens, and a scarf.

What would you say to me? Outwardly, you might ask, "Why are you so bundled up?" Inwardly, you'd probably think, "What's wrong with her?!"

My response: "Oh, I know it's hot out now, but it'll be cold in January, so I'm just getting prepared." Your reaction? "This shrink is crazy! I need to get out of here."

In most situations, wearing a winter coat when it's already hot makes no sense. And yet we often do something very similar when it comes to our thinking. Worrying about the future, and *emotionally reacting as if what we fear will occur is imminent*, is analogous to wearing your winter coat in the summer. You make yourself miserable anticipating the event, and you don't necessarily even fare better for the "preparation."

BTP TIP: Take Off That Winter Coat

When you notice that worry is starting to take over, remind yourself: "Don't put your winter coat on in the summer."

"But wait," my clients say, "isn't it important to think about worst-case scenarios so you can plan for them?"

Absolutely! That's analogous to making sure you have a winter coat in the closet. You have it for when you need it, but you don't wear it until it's called for. We'll discuss ways to do that in the Action Steps section.

In my clinical practice, I find that many perfectionists have superstitious thoughts about worrying. In addition to the idea that worrying helps us prepare for the worst-case scenario, two other superstitious statements I often hear are:

- ◆ "If I worry, then it won't happen."

- ◆ "If I worry, at least I'm doing *something*."

This first one is what I refer to as Umbrella Syndrome, the notion that "if I bring an umbrella, it won't rain." In reality there is no evidence to support this. In fact, the opposite may even be true (as some of us know all too well).

The second thought, the concept that doing something is at least better than doing nothing, is also not true. That's analogous to pushing on a bruise: it causes more pain, and it prevents healing rather than aiding it.

Rather than worrying about something, take steps to address it directly, using the problem-focused (working to change the situation) and/or emotion-focused (working to lessen your distress) approaches we talked about in Chapter 6: "Evaluate Your Expectations."

I'm not advocating that we all "think only happy thoughts." It's not a Pollyanna worldview we're after. We do, however, want to make sure our thoughts are *helpful*. That's why it's important to examine not only how accurate your superstitious thinking might be, but also how useful or beneficial it is to you.

So, do yourself (and those around you) a favor: don't wear your winter coat in the summer.

Worrying about the future is like wearing your winter coat in the summer.

ACTION STEPS: ADOPT REALISTIC OPTIMISM

Step 1: *Ditch Your Distortions*

Step 2: *Forge New Roads*

Step 3: *Rinse and Repeat!*

When I was a kid, I used to love to put on my dad's glasses, which had big, brown plastic frames (it was the seventies, after all). I'd then check out my new look in front of the mirror. The prescription was so strong I needed to peer over the frames in order to see myself clearly. Looking through the lenses just made everything very blurry.

Step 1: Ditch Your Distortions

Have you ever put on a pair of someone else's prescription glasses? If so, what you saw was likely somewhat askew. Remember, in Chapter 4: "Fear Versus Passion," how we imagined wearing blue-tinted glasses and seeing only green bananas? As in that example, we each view the world through our own psychological lens. And the way we see the world can be distorted without our even realizing it—the equivalent of not realizing you're wearing someone else's glasses.

What are some specific examples of distortions? All-or-nothing thinking, a cornerstone of perfectionism, is one type of distortion. We'll discuss this more in Chapter 9: "Eliminate Extremes."

Here are some additional common perfectionist cognitive distortions:

SAMPLE: COMMON PERFECTIONIST COGNITIVE DISTORTIONS

DISTORTION	WHAT IT IS	WHAT IT SOUNDS LIKE
Overgeneralizing	You establish a global pattern of negative events based on one occurrence.	• "Everyone lets me down." • "This never works for me." • "People always talk behind my back." • "I mess up every time."
Negative Filtering	You focus almost exclusively on the negatives without acknowledging any positives.	• "Look at all the bad things in my life. My life sucks." • "He doesn't help out around the house." • "My relationship is a mess." • "My body is disappointing."
Mind-Reading	You assume you know what people think without concrete proof.	• "She thinks I can't do it." • "He doesn't love me." • "He doesn't think I can do this." • "She thinks I am making this up."

▶

DISTORTION	WHAT IT IS	WHAT IT SOUNDS LIKE
Fortune-telling	You predict the future negatively, and emotionally react as if it's true.	• "I won't find true love." • "Things will just get worse." • "I am going to completely screw up." • "I won't get hired."
Catastrophizing	You interpret the past or predict the future in extreme terms—making mountains out of molehills.	• "It would be terrible if I messed up." • "I ruined everything." • "This is horrible." • "My job is a disaster."
Judgment Focus	You evaluate people and events in terms of being good or bad, positive or negative, instead of merely accepting or understanding the objective facts.	• "My presentation was crappy." • "He's a loser." • "She is stuck up." • "My life is pathetic. I am pathetic."
Regret Orientation	You focus on your "inadequacies" of the past instead of your competencies of the present.	• "He could have offered to help me." • "I shouldn't have done that." • "If only I had said that." • "I wish she had been more helpful when I was growing up."

As you can see, it's very easy to develop distorted perspectives. We all do it! But that doesn't mean we have to continue viewing our world this way. And the first step for altering our inaccurate views is to identify the particular ways we employ the different distortions above.

So now it's your turn. Read each distortion in the table below. Then, add at least one example of each from your own life. In fact, add as many as you can think of. We won't be able to take off our distorted glasses—to no longer see the world in an unrealistically positive or negative way—if we don't know we're wearing them.

EXERCISE: COMMON PERFECTIONIST COGNITIVE DISTORTIONS

DISTORTION	WHAT IT IS	WHAT IT SOUNDS LIKE	EXAMPLES FROM YOUR LIFE
Overgeneralizing	You establish a global pattern of negative events based on one occurrence.	• "Everyone lets me down." • "This never works for me." • "People always talk behind my back." • "I mess up every time."	
Negative Filtering	You focus almost exclusively on the negatives without acknowledging any positives.	• "Look at all the bad things in my life. My life sucks."	

▶

DISTORTION	WHAT IT IS	WHAT IT SOUNDS LIKE	EXAMPLES FROM YOUR LIFE
Negative Filtering (continued)	You focus almost exclusively on the negatives without acknowledging any positives.	• "He doesn't help out around the house." • "My relationship is a mess." • "My body is disappointing."	
Mind Reading	You assume you know what people think without concrete proof.	• "She thinks I can't do it." • "He doesn't love me." • "He doesn't think I can do this." • "She thinks I am making this up."	
Fortune-telling	You predict the future negatively, and emotionally react as if it's true.	• "I won't find true love." • "Things will just get worse." • "I am going to completely screw up." • "I won't get hired."	
Catastrophizing	You interpret the past or predict the future in extreme terms—making mountains out of molehills.	• "It would be terrible if I messed up." • "I ruined everything."	

▶

DISTORTION	WHAT IT IS	WHAT IT SOUNDS LIKE	EXAMPLES FROM YOUR LIFE
Catastrophizing *(continued)*	You interpret the past or predict the future in extreme terms—making mountains out of molehills.	• "This is horrible." • "My job is a disaster."	
Judgment Focus	You evaluate people and events in terms of being good or bad, positive or negative, instead of merely accepting or understanding the objective facts.	• "My presentation was crappy." • "He's a loser." • "She is stuck up." • "My life is pathetic. I am pathetic."	
Regret Orientation	You focus on (your) "inadequacies" of the past instead of (your) competencies of the present.	• "He could have offered to help me." • "I shouldn't have done that." • "If only I had said that." • "I wish she had been more helpful when I was growing up."	

"The need for change bulldozed a road down the center of my mind."
—MAYA ANGELOU

A CLIENT ONCE told me, "I don't want to just pretend like there are no problems. That's unrealistic." But the thing is, I'm not suggesting we all avoid noticing anything negative. *That* would be unrealistic. I am suggesting that we view the world through clear lenses. Not rosy-tinted lenses. Not gray-tinted lenses. (And not bifocal pink-gray lenses!) Clear lenses.

BTP TIP: Check Your Chart!

It's one thing to determine our distortions upon later reflection. It's quite another to catch ourselves in the act. But the better you become at recognizing your distortions, the better you'll be at reducing tension—in yourself and with others.

I suggest that you print out and carry with you your completed Common Perfectionist Cognitive Distortions exercise above. Then, the next time you get upset about something—not just slightly irked, but actually upset—stop for a moment and pull out your chart. As calmly as you can, review the distortions and try to determine if any of them are in play. If so, stop and take a breath, and try to come up with new, clear-eyed thoughts to replace the distortions. This could save you from potentially saying or doing something you would later regret.

Step 2: Forge New Roads

Whenever you determine that your old road is not accurate or helpful—perhaps when distortions are coloring your thinking—it's time to get out your bulldozer and create another path. How? Simply reframe the thoughts that aren't working for you into ones that are both accurate and helpful. When coaching clients through this process, I have found the following worksheet to be extremely effective. To illustrate, let's use the example of Caroline from the beginning of the chapter.

SAMPLE: CAROLINE'S REFRAMED THOUGHTS

EVENT (WHAT HAPPENED)	FEELINGS	AUTOMATIC THOUGHTS	DISTORTIONS	NEW THOUGHTS
My children are more independent now and don't need me as much.	◆ Sad ◆ Lonely ◆ Scared ◆ Lost	◆ I have no purpose in life. ◆ My life is incomplete. ◆ I will never feel good.	◆ Over-generalizing ◆ Negative Filtering ◆ Fortune-telling ◆ Catastro-phizing	◆ I get to choose my purpose. ◆ Now is a time when I can focus on me and what I really want to do. ◆ I am excited about this new stage in my life with infinite possibilities.

So that's Caroline's situation. Now, select a distressing experience of your own to work on. Start completing a table of your own below, filling in just the first four columns: Event (What Happened), Feelings, Automatic Thoughts, and Distortions. (Later on you'll complete the last column.)

EXERCISE: REFRAMING YOUR THOUGHTS

EVENT (WHAT HAPPENED)	FEELINGS	AUTOMATIC THOUGHTS	DISTORTIONS	NEW THOUGHTS

Most likely your assessment above isn't as supportive and realistic as it could be. To help you instead identify new thoughts that are both helpful and accurate, answer the following "reframing" questions:

- "How do I *want* to see this situation?"

- "Are there other ways to interpret what happened? If so, what different possible interpretations can I come up with?"

- "How might someone I admire view this situation?"

- "What advice would I give a friend in the same situation?"

- "What positives (about me, others, or the situation) am I ignoring?"

- "How helpful is it for me to think like this?"

- "If I was feeling more relaxed, how might I view this?"

Here's the key to the process: you want your new thoughts to feel good. Don't worry—you don't have to believe them (yet). You just have to *want* to believe them.

Consider the following scenario:

A homeless man has been wearing a coat for the past three years—eating, sleeping, living in this coat. It has not been washed for over a thousand days.

Imagine what this coat smells like. Whew!

Now, if he took off that coat, would you put it on? Assuming you wouldn't freeze to death without it, would you ever, ever, put on that coat?

Of course not!

And yet, that is exactly what we do when negative thoughts preoccupy our minds. Our distorted thinking is like wearing a stinky coat—a very stinky coat.

Why not take off that odorous outerwear? Why not put on a new coat?

What if, instead of this smelly jacket, you donned a beautiful, custom-made coat? The material—maybe cashmere, silk, or leather—feels glorious, and the jacket fits perfectly. In fact, it fits so well you think, "I never want to take this off!"

Your new thoughts are this custom-made coat. And they feel so good you can't believe you never have to take them off. Lucky you, because you can keep them on forever.

"A man is but a product of his thoughts: What he thinks, he becomes."

—GANDHI

Now, return to your table and complete the final column: New Thoughts. If you have trouble with the distortions, feel free to review the table of cognitive distortions in Step 1. If you have trouble coming up with new thoughts, review Caroline's example. (Think cashmere. Think silk.)

Step 3: Rinse and Repeat!

After you've identified new, helpful thoughts, it's time to make them stick. We want to make these new, positive thought pathways the *automatic* paths of least resistance—the ones you travel over and over, embedding them more and more deeply. We want to move them from temporary conscious thoughts to established subconscious beliefs. How? By using some of the same concepts in the beginning of this chapter.

There are two components to developing new pathways:

- Take the path repeatedly.

- Add weight as we traverse it.

To develop new thoughts, then, we need to:

- Repeat the new thoughts as frequently as possible.

- Use emotional weight to our advantage.

To do the first component—repeat the new thoughts—try using a variety of means of communication, such as:

- *Cognitive.* Think your new thoughts.

- *Written.* Write out your new thoughts over and over again.

- *Verbal.* Say your new thoughts out loud.

- *Mannerisms.* Use your body language to act *as if* your new thoughts are true.

- *Imagery.* Visualize what life would be like *if* you already believed these thoughts.

Regarding mannerisms: when we act as if something is true, we start to believe it more and more. If your new thought is "I can handle anything," then start holding your body the way someone who truly believes that statement would. Stand tall, hold your head up high, put a smile on your face, even try a swagger in your step. Research shows that how you hold your body can influence how you think. For example, in an Ohio State University study, the participants in a job interview who were instructed to sit up tall had more confidence and stronger belief in their skills than those who were told to slouch.

"Every time you are tempted to react in the same old way, ask if you want to be a prisoner of the past or a pioneer of the future."
—DEEPAK CHOPRA

Another powerful way to forge new pathways is through imagery or visualization, which helps spark the subconscious. Close your eyes and imagine that you completely believe your new thought. What does life look like? How do you act? How do others react to you? How do you interact with others? What types of things do you say to yourself and do? How do you feel? What is your body doing? Really allow yourself to experience the sensations.

This last part is key. Since using emotions to your advantage can help deepen neural pathways, they play a key role in incorporating your new thoughts into strongly held beliefs. So, imagine that this new positive thought about yourself—which you now think and write and say out loud and embody in your mannerisms—is indeed true. Let yourself *feel* the emotions and physical sensations you would *if* you believed it 100 percent. If you do this often enough, that image can become reality.

For a more in-depth example of a visualization, see Chapter 11: "Transcend."

BTP TIP: Smile!

Your body language doesn't just communicate to others; it also communicates to your brain. For example, we know that when we experience something that makes us happy, we smile. When this happens particular neural pathways fire up; consider this the "I'm happy, so I'm smiling" path through your open field.

Fortunately, it's possible to use this concept to our advantage. Essentially, we can walk that path starting from either end. Should you make yourself smile even without feeling particularly happy, the physical mannerism of the smile sends a message to your brain that says: "Hey, I'm smiling. I must feel happy." And you feel a little happier as a result.

In one research study, people who were smiling (even without realizing they were) while reading cartoons later reported having had more fun than did people who watched the same cartoons with a frown.

So use this concept to your advantage. If you want to feel happier, smile and laugh as much as you can, even when—especially when—you're not feeling happy. Work that path from both ends!

How would you feel if you truly believed your new thoughts?

◆ Happy?	◆ Blissful?	◆ Forgiving?
◆ Relieved?	◆ Excited?	◆ Motivated?
◆ Elated?	◆ Loving?	◆ Inspired?
◆ Powerful?	◆ Proud?	◆ Daring?
◆ Hopeful?	✳◆ Satisfied?	◆ Energetic?
◆ Pleased?	◆ Confident?	◆ Kindhearted?
◆ Eager?	◆ Determined?	

Whenever you repeat the new thought using any or all of the communication styles, try to let yourself fully experience your desired emotions.

To help you with the "Rinse and Repeat!" step—walking your new path often enough for it to have lasting effects—you might try mapping out a schedule for yourself. Here's what Caroline charted out:

SAMPLE: CAROLINE'S NEW ROADS

THIS WEEK, I WILL FOCUS ON MAKING THE FOLLOWING NEW THOUGHT A BELIEF.	Now is a time when I can focus on me and what I really want to do.
I will do this by . . .	*Visualizing what my life would be like if I took this time for myself.*
When	When I first wake up
How often	At least three times each week
I will remember to do this by	Putting a reminder next to my alarm clock
I will do this by . . .	*Saying the thought out loud in front of a mirror.*
When	When I brush my teeth
How often	Twice a day
I will remember to do this by	Putting a sticky note on the mirror in my bathroom

▶

THIS WEEK, I WILL FOCUS ON MAKING THE FOLLOWING NEW THOUGHT A BELIEF.	Now is a time when I can focus on me and what I really want to do.
I will do this by . . .	*Repeating the thought to myself.*
When	Throughout the day
How often	Five times
I will remember to do this by	Setting a reminder on my phone

Now it's your turn. Consider one of the new thoughts you developed in the previous section. To help make it stick, complete the following table with what *you* are going to do to reinforce this new pathway.

EXERCISE: FORGING NEW ROADS

THIS WEEK, I WILL FOCUS ON MAKING THE FOLLOWING NEW THOUGHT A BELIEF.	
I will do this by . . .	*Visualizing what my life would be like if I took this time for myself.*
When	
How often	
I will remember to do this by	

▶

I will do this by . . .	*Saying the thought out loud in front of a mirror.*
When	
How often	
I will remember to do this by	
I will do this by . . .	*Repeating the thought to myself.*
When	
How often	
I will remember to do this by	

If you have trouble with this, try pretending you're an actor. The character you are playing truly believes your new thought is absolutely, 100 percent true. Now walk, talk, feel, act, and *be* this character. And enjoy the benefits of these new roads in your life!

CHAPTER 8

F: Fail Forward

*"The most valuable thing you can make is a mistake.
You can't learn anything from being perfect."*
—ADAM OSBORNE

ATYCHIPHOBIA IS THE intense fear of failure. Just the prospect of failing causes people with this disorder such dread and anxiety that they feel nauseated or sick. They sweat, experience heart palpitations, have difficulty speaking or thinking clearly, feel as if they're losing control, and may even have a full-blown panic attack. They try to avoid failing by any means. And yet, they are often aware that their overwhelming fear is not completely rational, since what they're so afraid of rarely poses any real threat.

While they may not meet all the criteria for the psychiatric diagnosis, most perfectionists have some level of atychiphobia. For perfectionists—and many with perfectionist tendencies—failure is equated with catastrophe and calamity, and must be avoided at all costs.

In reality, however, mistakes can be doorways to discovery.

In this chapter we will explore the concept of failing forward. The goal is to reframe the idea of "failure" and learn to embrace what previously scared the heck out of you. Let me show you how failing led one woman into a totally unexpected future for herself and others like her. By failing forward, she was able to use her passion to help her develop a remarkable plan for world peace.

> *Marilyn King was an Olympic athlete, a member of the U.S. team in the 1972 and 1976 Summer Olympic Games. She competed in the grueling pentathlon (hurdles, shot put, high jump, long jump, and an eight-hundred-meter sprint).*
>
> *While Marilyn was driving on the freeway one day in November 1979, a truck hit her car from behind. The accident left her unable to train for the 1980 Moscow Games, as she was now incapable of the necessary six- to eight-hour daily training sessions—sprinting, jumping, throwing, and weightlifting. She'd also lost the routine she'd maintained for twenty years.*
>
> *When I first met Marilyn, I found her piercing blue eyes captivating, but as she spoke, it was her story that kept me enthralled.*
>
> *When I asked how she'd gotten started as an Olympian, she chuckled. "In junior high I did track and field. I was*

pretty good, always came in second or third. And that was okay with me.

"Then the U.S. Olympic Committee invited someone I had beaten to go to the Olympic training camp. I thought, 'I know I'm better than her. If they think she can go to the Olympics, that means I can go to the Olympics.'

"It was a crazy idea and I kept it a secret. I didn't tell anyone but I could not get the thought out of my head. I thought about it every day."

And she made it happen.

Before school, after school, weekends, holidays, every possible moment was focused on envisioning being an Olympian and practicing every part of what it would take.

When you are passionate about something, nothing becomes too tough to solve, and Marilyn was a problem solver. No team for girls? No hurdles at the abandoned track she'd found to practice in? No problem. She had lightweight hurdles made from used pipes, marked the track with nail polish, and taped a flashlight to the curb so she could finish her workout after dark.

Her dedication paid off. In 1972 Marilyn made her first Olympic team, competing in Munich.

She described the experience of walking into the stadium. "My mouth just hung open. I was stunned. It was like nothing I had ever seen before." Feeling more like a spectator than an athlete competing against the far superior Russians and East

Germans, Marilyn vowed to return and be more competitive in the next Olympic Games.

She placed sixteenth in the 1976 Montreal Olympics. Though she was determined to compete one last time in Moscow, fate had other plans for her.

As Marilyn lay in bed after her car accident, she kept thinking, "I'll be in the top three at the Olympic trials and I'm getting better every day."

Weeks turned into months and she was no better. Ever the problem solver, Marilyn realized that, while she could not train physically for the Olympic trials, she could practice mentally. She trained mentally for seven months, both watching films of the world-record holders in all five events and standing on the track envisioning herself working on each of her events.

When the U.S. Olympic trials for the 1980 Moscow Summer Games came around, despite her lack of physical training, she placed second, beating all but one of the competitors for the U.S. team.

But Marilyn would not get to compete in the Games in 1980. No Americans did, due to a boycott by then-president Jimmy Carter in protest of the Soviet invasion of Afghanistan.

Of course Marilyn was deeply disappointed about not being able to participate in the Games. At the same time, she was dumbfounded by her accomplishment. "I was just an ordinary person who had something extraordinary happen that was impossible to explain."

Wanting to learn more, Marilyn quit her job coaching at UC Berkeley and spent three years researching the field of exceptional human performance.

Based on her 1980 experience, research, and collaboration with other Olympians, Marilyn came to realize, "There are three things that are always present when people achieve extraordinary things.

*"The first is **passion**. Successful people are passion-powered. It is never about things they 'should' do or are supposed to do. It's not willpower; it's 'want power.' Passion is what gets you out of bed, what makes you become a creative problem solver.*

*"The second is **vision**. High achievers think in a very particular way. I call it vision-guided. We all do it sometimes; Olympians do it every day.*

*"The third is **action**. Olympians and other high achievers are action-oriented. They have daily practices that move them step-by-step toward their goal. But not just physical practice; achieving at the highest level requires mental practice as well. Mental practice provides the critical difference for high-level success.*

"Altogether, top achievement requires an alignment of these three elements: passion, vision, and action. I call this trio 'Olympian Thinking.' And anyone, not just athletes, can apply it to whatever it is they want to achieve.

"When you apply Olympian Thinking to your own world, everything changes: how you think, what you think about

*your job, your relationships, your day, your life. It's called
'disruptive technology.' But, most importantly, you can apply
Olympian Thinking to the wider world as well, contributing
to a world that works for all."*

Marilyn is convinced that this disruptive technology will
literally accelerate the next evolution of peace across our
entire planet. *"When people change what I call their 'stink-
ing thinking' about peace—that it can't be achieved, that it's
a lost cause, that we can't because . . . —and realize that it is
possible when we apply Olympian Thinking, we can accelerate the shift of humanity up one level from 'relative peace,'
where most people now live, to what I call 'sweet peace.'*

*"People tend to be poorly informed, misinformed, and
have beliefs based on partial information shaped by the traditional media that primarily highlights the problems. When
people become fully informed and see the whole truth, the
unprecedented level of global cooperation, problem-solving,
and best-practices sharing humankind is currently experiencing, they begin to switch their thinking from 'Can't be done'
to 'Wow, maybe this can be done.' That's when people begin
to think more effectively and creatively about what they can
do to be part of the shift. They begin to fine-tune their daily
actions to contribute to the almost universal desire for peace.*

*"By aligning the three elements of Olympian Thinking—
passion, vision, and daily action—we can achieve our personal
dreams and fulfill our common dream of peace."*

Marilyn's mission, with Olympians worldwide as messengers, is to make Olympian Thinking available to youth everywhere to positively impact their personal lives, their local communities, and the world we all want to live in.

While some may have seen a debilitating car accident as a huge obstacle to an Olympic pursuit, Marilyn found other powerful ways to train. Failing forward not only allowed her to place second at the trials for her third Olympics, but also launched her on the road to discover and share how we can all be part of bringing peace to our world.

Mistakes can be doorways to discovery.

ALL FAILURE IS BAD—OR IS IT?

While it may seem that perfectionists crave perfection, their main motivation is often not the desire to be "perfect," but rather the desire to not fail. That fear is central. Constantly worried about failure, perfectionists devote hours of mental and physical energy to prevent it. As we discussed in Chapter 4: "Fear Versus Passion," it's the opposite of being motivated by passion. Instead of being propelled toward something they want, they strive to reduce the pain they fear is coming their way.

Stop and think about the difference for a moment. While this distinction may seem like just semantics, it results in totally different lives.

For one thing, trying to minimize what we don't want creates more negative energy. We worry about what will occur, obsess about what to do if the worst happens, and second-guess our decisions; essentially, we stress out. This can lead to some unfortunate old companions: burnout, anxiety, insomnia, depression, and a whole host of other issues.

"Success is a lousy teacher. It seduces smart people into thinking they can't lose."
—BILL GATES

In contrast, focusing on what we *do* want can help motivate and inspire us to make positive change, not because we "have" to, but rather because we *want* to. Here, the energy is more positive, affirming, and constructive. Hope, resilience, and empowerment prevail when we focus on working toward a beneficial goal.

Marilyn King's story embodies these powerful positive qualities. That's what makes her story so inspiring, isn't it? How different would your life look if you used Olympian Thinking on a daily basis?

"I've come to believe that all my past failure and frustration were actually laying the foundation for the understandings that have created the new level of living I now enjoy."
—TONY ROBBINS

PERFECTIONISTS OFTEN THINK they're moving toward what they want when in actuality they're focused on avoiding their biggest fear: messing up and having their "failure" seen by others.

Interestingly, though, what may have been perceived as failures can turn into huge wins.

Consider the Slinky. Chances are you're familiar with this flexible springlike toy, and have seen it "walk" down stairs. Millions have played with this . . . "failure." In 1943, a mechanical engineer was trying to create stabilizers to keep fragile equipment from falling and breaking on ships. The springs he came up with did not work. They did, however, make a fun toy!

Have you ever watched the animated film *Toy Story*? This Academy Award–winning film and many others like it wouldn't have existed if not for a failure. After being famously fired from Apple, the company he'd cofounded, Steve Jobs acquired an animation studio that he turned into Pixar Animation Studios. Since then, Pixar has produced fourteen feature films, won twenty-seven Academy Awards, and earned over $8 billion, including over $1 billion from *Toy Story 3*.

Then there was Nicole Kidman's marriage "failure." In 2001 she and Tom Cruise, her husband of eleven years, divorced. Though she won an Academy Award two years later, the loss of her marriage dampened the enjoyment of her professional victory. In an interview in *Marie Claire*, Kidman said, "I was really damaged and not sure whether that was ever going to happen again to me. I certainly never thought I'd have a baby at forty-one. But we never know what's around the corner."

Years later she said in an interview with *Vanity Fair,* "With no disrespect to what I had with Tom, I've met my great love now." It took her painful experiences to help her find true love and happiness.

EXERCISE: REFRAMING "FAILURE"

In looking back over your own experiences, has a seeming "failure" in your life ever turned into a positive result, or even a true blessing? Describe the experience here.

_____

_____

_____

_____

_____

_____

_____

When was a time when you thought you had failed, only to later see things differently?

_____

_____

_____

_____

_____

_____

_____

▶

Have you ever lost your job, only to find a better one? Describe what took place.

_____

_____

_____

_____

_____

_____

_____

Have you ever lost a relationship that was important to you, and then later found an even better match? What happened?

_____

_____

_____

_____

_____

_____

_____

"Strength does not come from winning. Your struggles develop your strengths. When you go through hardships and decide not to surrender, that is strength."

—ARNOLD SCHWARZENEGGER

BEFORE BECOMING A psychologist, I was a physical therapist. During my training as a PT, I learned that, in order to grow muscles, you actually have to break them down first. Lifting weights, for example, causes the muscle to contract. When the weight becomes an overload for the muscles (from the actual weight or the frequency of repetitions), some of the muscle's tissue fibers tear. In essence, part of the muscle "fails" from the overload.

When you rest, these muscles rebuild themselves to be stronger than before. This type of failure is *required* for the muscles to build up.

In the same way, failure can be a tool for further success, if we let it be.

WHAT DOES FEAR OF FAILURE LOOK LIKE?

For a perfectionist, the fear of failure can rear its head in seemingly contradictory approaches:

- Risk Aversion

- Excessive Energy

- Indecisiveness

Let's look at how each one can show up in our lives.

Risk Aversion

Those who are "risk-averse" avoid situations they fear will result in failure. They may procrastinate on a task for as long as possible, or they may avoid the task completely. While many might feel some trepidation about concerns of a financial or psychological nature, for perfectionists risk aversion can also extend into relationships, health, even leisure time. Imagine someone wanting to get in a swimming pool. It's safer to know what you're getting into—to dip your toe in the shallow end of a pool, testing the water—than it is *not* to know and just jump in the deep end . . . only to find it's a *really* deep end. While swimming in that pool might be really fun, might even bring great happiness, for some the potential dangers aren't worth the risk.

"The biggest risk is not taking any risk. . . .
In a world that's changing really quickly, the
only strategy that is guaranteed to fail is not
taking risks."
—MARK ZUCKERBERG

Romantic relationships are a great example of this.

"I am never going to get myself in that situation again," Katy sobbed, overwhelmed by tears.

Katy was telling me how her husband of seventeen years had shocked her six months earlier, telling her, "I'm not in love with you anymore. I want out of this marriage."

"I felt like my entire world was crumbling," she said. "First he wants to leave me. Then I find out he's been having an affair with some woman from work who is ten years younger than me. It's so cliché.

"How could this happen to me?! I trusted him. I took care of him. I did everything for him. And this is how he treats me.

"I still feel sick to my stomach. I have trouble sleeping. I feel like such a loser. I am never, ever, going to put myself in a place of such vulnerability again.

"My friends keep asking when I'm going to get out there and start dating. I can tell you this—I have no desire to ever again be in the position where I cared so much for someone and he stomped all over my heart."

Can you relate? Do you:

- Keep others at a distance because you're afraid they will hurt you?

- Avoid getting close to someone for fear it will ruin your relationship?

- Not embark upon a task because you worry it will result in failure?

- Stay away from activities that interest you because you're convinced you'll fail at them?

- Fear (or even avoid) success, thinking it will ultimately lead to failure?

Talk about risk aversion! For a perfectionist, certainty outweighs a gamble, even when that certainty is less desirable than what the gamble offers. The result? A life that is less fulfilling than it could be.

BTP TIP: Take a Risk in Love

Being vulnerable in a relationship is vital to developing deeper bonds. Sure, it may be scary at first. But, instead of worrying that your vulnerability will come back to bite you, try to focus on how being the true you will help you both become closer. And be on the lookout for distorted thinking, especially all-or-nothing thinking. (See "Sample: Common Perfectionist Cognitive Distortions" in Chapter 7.) Ease into it. When you take a chance dipping your feet into cold water, the longer you stay in the water, the more you acclimate to its temperature. So, too, can you become more comfortable with taking calculated risks in a relationship.

Now let's look at ways risk aversion can present itself in our professional lives.

Have you ever:

- Declined a job promotion for fear you couldn't handle the responsibilities of the new job?

- Not volunteered for a project that would have been great for your career for fear you'd "fail"?

- Not even bothered to apply for a position or program because you felt you couldn't handle being rejected for it?

- Avoided starting a project for fear you wouldn't do it well enough?

- Put off doing something because you were afraid you'd fail?

- Procrastinated on a task even though putting it off created additional stress?

Sometimes people label tasks they think will result in failure as a "waste of time."

"It never works for me," Scott grumbled. "It's just a complete waste of time."

At forty-seven years old, the six-foot-three gentleman with salt-and-pepper hair looked as if he hadn't had a good night's sleep in weeks. In fact, he hadn't.

Formerly employed as an attorney in a relatively large firm, Scott had lost his job three months earlier. This father of four had sunken into a deep funk: his mood was low, he no longer enjoyed his favorite activities (like spending time with his children), he lacked motivation, and he had feelings of hopelessness.

Scott had trouble even getting out of bed in the morning. In fact, sitting with him in my office, noting his disheveled hair, I wondered if he'd even bathed in the last couple of days.

It is extremely common for unemployment to trigger depression. While being unemployed certainly has financial repercussions, for many people it's also a huge psychological struggle. People often equate who they are with what they do. Take away the job, and you take away their sense of self.

Scott and I had been focusing on steps he could take to find another job. During this session we were discussing networking.

According to the U.S. Bureau of Labor Statistics, 70 percent of all jobs are found through networking. Still, many people, like Scott, avoid networking because it hasn't worked for them . . . yet.

Instead, he was sitting at his computer Googling job opportunities and applying to companies—adding his résumé to the thousands received for each position. Scott also spent a fair amount of time procrastinating on the Internet: reading about his favorite team, getting the latest news, and watching YouTube videos.

Can you relate?

"My mother always told me I wouldn't amount to anything because I procrastinate. I said, 'Just wait.'"

—JUDY TENUTA, ACTOR AND COMEDIAN

Ask yourself: what activities do I avoid that, if I actually did them, could ultimately bring me:

- Greater happiness?

- Improved health?

- Better relationships?

- Greater success at work?

- Financial gain?

- Spiritual wellness?

Consider for a minute: what would your life be like *if* you stopped running away and actually tackled the projects, faced the people, and took on the roles you've been avoiding?

During our session, we discussed how to change Scott's view of networking, that essential career activity he avoided because he'd convinced himself "it never works."

Instead, we reframed the purpose of networking from "getting a job" to "making new connections." Yes, these connections may help Scott find job opportunities. They may also serve other benefits, like developing a support network, finding new opportunities and resources, and discovering ways to help others.

The reframed goal was simply to connect with others—not in an "I got twenty-one business cards today" kind of way, but rather "I met three really interesting people today." In avoiding networking, Scott was denying himself opportunities to connect with others, which is a basic human need—one that would serve him far beyond his career interests.

Armed with this new perspective, Scott went to a networking event. He returned to see me the next week.

"I met this guy who just lost his job. Man, he was practically in tears. I pulled him to the side and told him I'd help him out. We met the next day and I rewrote his entire résumé.

"It was good to help someone else. It was also great to talk to a guy going through what I'm going through—trying to find a job and support my family, with a wife who is nagging me about getting a job, and me feeling like my balls have been cut off. His wife nags him even more than mine, poor guy."

BTP TIP: Make Networking Work for You

Reframing the purpose of networking, as Scott did, can help you optimize your efforts. Here are three additional tips to help make networking work for you:

+ *Focus on giving rather than getting.* Not only will helping someone else boost your own happiness and increase your confidence, research shows it will also prime people to want to help you in return.

+ *Introduce others.* When you introduce other people, you claim a leader's position in helping both parties. It's a two-for-one deal.

+ *Follow up.* Follow-ups might include sending your new contact an interesting article, asking how the important meeting went, or scheduling another time to get together. This extra effort not only makes you more memorable, it does so in a positive manner.

When we avoid risk, we keep ourselves out of many "games"—refusing even to set foot on the field. While no one wants to fail, this protective mechanism we use is overly protective, and prevents us from living life fully.

Is that worth it to you?

One more comment about risk aversion: the purpose of procrastination and avoidance is to put off what you fear or dread, having determined that "it's too stressful to deal with now." Ironically, though, procrastination and avoidance actually *increase* your stress. The thought "I need to do that" will continue to weigh you down until you finally attend to the task. Avoidance and procrastination can actually cause more of what you're trying to reduce—perhaps even adding unpleasant consequences to boot.

Excessive Energy

In contrast to risk aversion, many perfectionists instead focus on or even reside at the other end of the spectrum: excessive work.

I had just given a talk in front of a couple of hundred people about bringing happiness into the workplace. I shared how research indicates that happier employees are more resilient, use less health care, are more productive, and help make much more money for their company. Ah, but I digress.

After watching my presentation and connecting with the message, Gretchen approached me, saying, "I need help with public speaking."

When we met for our first session, she explained what she meant. Turned out that Gretchen was pretty amazing on-stage—she'd sent me some videos to give me a sense of what we'd be addressing.

"People always tell me what a great speaker I am," she said. "Even so, I am scared to death of failing. I mean, what if I get onstage and forget what I was supposed to say? What if my slides don't work? What if I trip on my way to the stage? What if I totally screw up?!"

By now, Gretchen had worked herself into a state of panic. Just thinking about the possibility of what she called "failing" was enough. Her fear was almost palpable: her eyes were wide open, and the muscles in her hands and neck were tight. It was so intense I noticed my own stress level rising!

"What do you do to feel less stressed?" I asked Gretchen.

"Practice. I practice my speech over and over."

Certainly practice can be a good thing when it comes to giving a speech. For Gretchen, though, it was causing her more stress.

"Give me a sense of what that practice entails," I asked her.

"Well, for every presentation I give, I practice between fifty and seventy-five times. And when I say 'practice,' I mean I do the entire presentation—all sixty minutes of it—about fifty to seventy-five times."

Given that, on average, Gretchen gave a speech once every two months, that was a lot of practicing. And this extensive preparation was entirely driven by her fear of failing.

But Gretchen conceded that her approach wasn't entirely helpful to her. The long hours brought with them a lot of consequences. "It puts a lot of strain on my marriage," she said. "Not only the time I spend, but also the stress I have.

"And I can't sleep very well for about a week before, which I know is bad for my health."

With further consideration, Gretchen said, "You know, I wonder if all that practice actually makes the speech worse. I never thought of it before, but the excessive practice may make me more stressed and less effective."

She figured out that, instead of worrying about saying every word she had scripted, having the general concepts in her head and practicing communicating them was much more effective—and healthier.

"What if," I asked, "you were able to get rid of your fear of failure? What if, instead, you could just focus on getting the message out to help as many people as possible?"

So Gretchen tried that. Every time her fear of failure reared its ugly head, she focused on what she wanted her audience to gain. She also gave herself a break and became more relaxed.

BTP TIP: A "Perfect" Speech Can Be Boring!

Pay close attention to conversations you have with friends and family. Notice how often they forget a word, have difficulty explaining something, or pause while they're speaking in a relaxed manner. This is completely normal. So when you're onstage or feeling nervous about speaking, give yourself a break. It's okay if you don't say the "perfect" word, or if you need to take a moment to think.

Plus, perfect is boring, especially in front of an audience. A perfectly delivered speech may feel inauthentic or seem too rehearsed. The best way to get your information across is to be yourself and speak from the heart.

Here's another important point that often gets forgotten by perfectionists: busy does not equal productive. Sometimes doing more results in a better outcome. But sometimes the physical and mental energy you put into being busy actually prevents an optimal performance.

Busy does not equal productive.

Indecisiveness

A *Today Show* interview I did while writing this book speaks so beautifully about how rampant perfectionism is and how it affects our ability to make decisions. Perfectionists second-guess themselves, often agonizing over making the "right" decision. Unable to make and stick with a decision, they experience "analysis paralysis." Here's a portion:

> *"A comment on our Facebook page was interesting,"* Hoda Kotb, *one of the co-anchors of* The Today Show, *told me. "One woman said, 'One of my biggest obstacles is I'm never able to make decisions for myself . . . even little stuff.'"*
>
> Kathie Lee Gifford: *"Well, what makes you indecisive? It's fear, right?"*
>
> I answered: *"Yes, it is fear of making a mistake, so just go with it [your decision]."*
>
> Kathie: *"But how do you just tell yourself to just go with it? Fear is a very real thing to people."*
>
> *"Fear is real,"* I responded. *"And the best way to overcome your fear is to face it. We are such a perfectionistic society, thinking 'Oh, it has to be the perfect decision.' There is no 'perfect' decision. Make a decision; go with it. If it doesn't work out the way you want, then make a change later."*

Can you relate?

+ Do you ever have trouble making decisions for fear that you will make the "wrong" one?

◆ Do you ever feel practically paralyzed by fear that you don't
   know what the "right" decision is?

◆ Do you ever second-guess yourself?

Maybe your indecisiveness is related to:

◆ What to wear

◆ What project to start

◆ What to serve for dinner

Okay, so these are some areas where I sometimes have trouble
making decisions . . .

Here's the deal: there is no *one* right way that makes all the other
ways wrong. There are so many ways to do something. And most decisions we make are not life-and-death important. Remember the brain
surgeon in Chapter 1? Okay, his ability to operate on somebody's
brain *is* life or death. But deciding whether to wear the red jacket or
the blue dress to the office tomorrow—not so much.

The key is to look at the information you have and make the best
decision you can make *at that time*. If it turns out not to work:

✓ Don't personalize it. An undesired result does not mean you're
   a failure at making decisions.

✓ Forgive yourself. Stop beating yourself up about it.

✓ Remember: you made the best decision you could at that particular time with the information that was available then.

✓ Choose a new path using the new information you now have.

This third point is really key. Ever heard the term "Monday morning quarterbacking"? It refers to people who judge what a football team *should* have done instead of what actually happened. So, after a quarterback's throw gets intercepted someone might say, "He should have run the ball." Yes, it may be true that that would have been a better approach, given what actually happened. But that's 20-20 hindsight, isn't it? After all, there's a good chance his play would have worked out well.

Have you ever played the lottery? If so, have you ever looked at the winning number the next day and thought, "I should have known that!" Probably not, because there's no way you could have known what the winning number would end up being.

Similarly, when you make a decision, you base it on the information you have right now. Any new information you get later may determine whether it was an effective decision. But right now, trust yourself—believe in yourself—and have confidence you can use the information you have now to make the best choice you can.

BTP TIP: Simplify Decision-Making

When making a decision, consider the steps my mentors, Arthur Nezu, PhD, and Christine Maguth Nezu, PhD, teach. Determine how this decision:

- Actually solves the problem

- Affects you (emotionally, physically, time spent, effort needed, etc.)

- Affects others (loved ones, society, environment)

- Plays out in the short term

- Plays out in the long term

You might find this checklist simplifies things a great deal.

*You make the best decisions you can with the
information that is available at that time.*

It is important to give yourself a break. Now let's look at how perfectionists react when it is someone else who "fails" them.

WHEN THINGS GO WRONG

*It was the last month of seventh grade. The Connecticut snow
had melted, and spring was in the air. The birds and the bees
were swarming.*

*My BFF, Kim, and I spent a lot of our free time together.
Every evening we would chat on the phone for hours. Fridays
after school, we would walk downtown and eat pizza. Weekend nights we'd sleep over at each other's houses. I remember
one Saturday night staying up until well past two in the morning trying to write down every word in the lyrics of "Jack and
Diane" by John Cougar Mellencamp.*

*I was overweight in seventh grade. When I was younger,
there was a "no candy" rule in my house. So with the new-
found freedom I had in middle school, I rebelled and de-
voured candy whenever I could get my hands on some.*

*One day while at school, I learned that there was a party
happening in two weeks. It was a boy-girl party. And I was
not invited.*

It felt as if I had been sucker punched out of the blue.

Then it got worse. It was Kim, my supposed best friend, who was hosting the party. Another knockout jab while I was already down.

I felt dejected and rejected. Sulking, I tried to avoid my friends, all of whom seemed to have been invited to the coed festivities.

Eventually, I got up the nerve to ask Kim, "How come you didn't invite me?"

Kim looked at me with what I now believe was true kindness in her heart and said, "I thought you'd be too embarrassed to go." As she made this statement, she looked down at my waist.

Devastated that someone whom I trusted so much had completely rejected me—in my mind—I felt like an absolute failure. How could I be such a loser and not even realize it?

Can you relate?

Whenever something hurts or disappoints us, we process it in our minds, trying to understand why it happened. And we process information through the filter of how we view things: through whatever schema we may have. (We talked about schemas in the last chapter.) My schema in this example is that a BFF invites you to her parties. But when real-life data contradict our blueprint, our worldview, it's distressing and confusing.

Before this event, my belief about friends was: they can be trusted and they want to help you. Kim was a friend, so I assumed that she could be trusted and that she wanted what was best for me.

When she didn't invite me to what I was convinced was the party of the century, my thoughts were, "Kim did this behind my back. She made a fool out of me. Everyone is laughing at me. I am a failure."

Looking back, the above description is not at all what I now think was actually going on. At the time, though, this was my conviction 100 percent.

In psychology we call the stress we feel when reality does not match our beliefs cognitive dissonance. Cognitive dissonance is very stressful, and we often subconsciously take steps to get rid of it. We do this in two different ways: accommodation and assimilation.

When we *accommodate*, we change our established schema so that the incongruous new data make sense. When we *assimilate*, we alter the incongruous information in order to fit it into our established belief patterns. Let's look at these cognitive actions in terms of the scenario of being excluded from Kim's party.

Using assimilation, I would have said, "If Kim is a friend, and friends can be trusted and only want what's best for me, then I must have done something wrong. It must be my fault that the friendship failed. If only I was not so fat, then she never would have done this to me. I am a failure."

With assimilation, I'd consider my definition of a friend to still be true. So when my interpretation of reality did not jibe with my concept of a friend, I would change how I interpreted what happened—that I was a failure.

BTP TIP: Reactions to Trauma

People who have experienced trauma frequently process the incident with the subconscious coping mechanism of assimilation or overaccommodation.

In the case of overaccommodation, someone who'd been in a car accident might develop a belief that it's not safe to ride in a car. Or someone who was molested may believe that no man can ever be trusted.

An example of assimilation would be when a woman in an abusive relationship blames herself for her partner's aggression. Her mind tells her: "If he loves me, and since people who love each other are not violent, then it must be that I'm doing something wrong to make him do this."

Beware of strong beliefs developed when tough circumstances take place. Make sure your beliefs are both accurate and helpful.

On the other hand, if I used accommodation, I would have instead changed my definition of friends. A healthy use of accommodation might have been something like, "Friends can be trusted sometimes but not always." Of course, when emotions are high, our thoughts are not always healthy or helpful. When the stress level is high, as it was in this case, overaccommodation can also occur.

Overaccommodation happens when you alter your worldview in an extreme manner so as to accommodate the extreme dissonance. The result? Thinking, for example, "I can trust no one." Clearly this new schema could have serious consequences on all future relationships.

But it's not as if we consciously choose one or the other response to cognitive dissonance. When it comes to making sense out of something upsetting, we might do a bit of both, which is what I did. In order to process not being invited to Kim's party, I concluded that "I was a failure because I was so fat" and that "I cannot trust others." I wasn't conscious of this perspective shift; it just made sense to me at the time.

Not wanting ever to feel that horrible again, I worked to prevent future failures by developing new ways to think and interact with others. I didn't trust people, and the friends I did have I avoided being intimate with. I also worked on losing weight in rather unhealthy ways, like skipping breakfast and lunch.

EXERCISE: RETHINKING WHEN THINGS GO WRONG

Think of times in your life when you've struggled to understand difficult failures. Can you think of times you've used assimilation: you reinterpreted what happened so it jibed with your prior beliefs? Or times you've used overaccommodation: drastically changing your entire view of someone, something, or a situation in order to make sense of what happened?

After being hurt in a relationship, did you make up a new rule, such as "No man can be trusted" or "All women are bad news"? Describe what happened.

_____

_____

_____

_____

_____

_____

_____

_____

_____

▶

When something upsetting happened in your life, did you beat yourself up for it, deciding you were "the reason" it happened? Describe how this felt.

_____

_____

_____

_____

_____

_____

_____

_____

Have you developed stringent explanations for past "failures" that you now use as laws, restricting how you act so you don't fail again? Describe your new rules.

_____

_____

_____

_____

_____

_____

_____

_____

ACTIONS STEPS: FAIL FORWARD

Step 1: *"Data" Versus "Failure"*

Step 2: *Forgive*

Step 3: *Identify Your Values*

Overcoming the fear of failure calls for changing our concept of what it means to fail. To do this, think about how some previous "failures" ultimately turned into blessings. Perhaps the end of a troubled relationship led you to finding a much more fulfilling love match. Or a lost job resulted in landing even better work. Start shifting your focus from your fears to your values and desires. Don't let fear define who you are. Let the true you shine through!

Step 1: "Data" Versus "Failure"

What if we could change your entire perspective about "failure"? What if, instead of seeing an event as a failure, you saw it instead as "data"?

I remember taking chemistry class in high school. My teacher would have us carry out certain experiments and document the results. Sometimes, our findings were consistent with what we predicted, and sometimes not. When my lab mates and I got an unanticipated outcome, we didn't think, "Ugh, what a failure." Instead, we were taught to ask, "Why did we get that result?"

To figure that out, we were taught to ask ourselves:

+ Did we follow the steps exactly?

+ What ingredients may have resulted in this outcome?

- Do we need to adjust any quantities or details?

- What other factors might have played a role?

In essence, we used the unexpected outcome as a source of data. This allowed us to learn from what happened and make adjustments in order to hopefully get a better outcome in the future. And that's not "failure"; that's the scientific method, pure and simple.

There are so many opportunities to use this concept in every aspect of your life: in relationships, health issues, work. For example, let's say a project you took on didn't turn out as you hoped. Instead of internalizing the "failure," what if you instead asked yourself the four "chemistry" questions above, walking yourself through the data to see if you can find any opportunities for improvement? I mean, when a company's sales are lower than expected, they don't dwell on the failure; they work to figure out how to improve next month's figures, right? Couldn't it be the same for you?

ACCEPTING "FEEDBACK" IS another great example of how this concept can be useful in our everyday lives. When a significant other, boss, friend, colleague, neighbor, or even a stranger tells a perfectionist something she doesn't want to hear, she tends to react in one of two ways:

- "He's right. I am a complete failure!"

- "He has no idea what he's talking about. Screw him!"

Can you relate?

What if, instead, you listened to the feedback and, as objectively as possible, determined how helpful it was? (Okay, I know that can be really hard sometimes, but stay with me here!) Try working under the assumption that this person comes from a good place and doesn't want to hurt you. Then ask yourself these questions:

- If this were true, what would that mean?

- How can I use this information to improve myself?

- Is it possible that he sees this as truth, even though I do not? And if so, what steps can I take to better communicate with this person?

Rather than judging what happened or what was said as a failure and beating yourself up about it, use the situation as *data* to motivate you to reach a better conclusion next time.

BTP TIP: Why Do People Give "Feedback"?

Ever wonder why people give negative feedback? Is what they say true? Or, are they trying to put you down?

Before we answer that question, let's answer another one: what's in a chocolate cake? I know it may seem like a strange question, but work with me. What is in a chocolate cake?

Some of the ingredients are chocolate, sugar, butter, flour, eggs, and vanilla, right?

Okay, next question. Does flour alone make a chocolate cake? No. Do eggs by themselves make a chocolate cake? No.

You need all the ingredients mixed together and baked in a particular manner in order to get a chocolate cake.

What does a cake recipe have to do with anything someone says about you? When people do or say something, it is usually brought about by a number of ingredients. In the case of someone giving you feedback, they may be tired and irritable, so they focus on the negative. (Remember, our brains tend toward a negative bias.) Or they ▶

may truly want to help you be even better at what you do. Or maybe you remind them of someone from their past, which colors their interactions with you. It could be all of these and so much more.

So when someone's feedback gets you down, keep in mind that a combination of different ingredients are likely at play. You might find that you can use some of what's happened as data, which you can utilize in the future if you choose. Try not to personalize their behavior; the majority of it most likely has *nothing* to do with you.

Step 2: Forgive

Forgiveness is a complicated concept that can mean different things to different people. In psychology, *forgiveness* refers to releasing anger and resentment about something that happened in the past. When it comes to forgiving yourself, it means letting go of the guilt and shame you feel.

When we hold on to grudges, essentially we're wishing the outcome had been different. In fact, not forgiving is often motivated by a strong desire to have gotten a different result. In reality, of course, we cannot go back in time and change what happened. We have no control over what has already taken place. In an attempt to overcome that powerlessness, though, we often berate ourselves or others, thinking, "If only X had happened instead, then things would be better."

Forgiveness is crucial to failing forward because (1) forgiveness removes the judgment, the sense of "failure"; (2) without forgiveness we're stuck in the past; and (3) forgiveness allows us to learn from the past.

How do you forgive? The key is understanding what forgiveness is and what it is not. Many people don't understand what forgiveness actually involves, which often prevents them from benefitting from it.

*"I believe that every single event in life happens in
an opportunity to choose love over fear."*
—OPRAH

Forgiveness is *not*:

- Condoning or justifying what happened

- Saying it was not a big deal

- Letting the other person (or yourself) off the hook

- Allowing it to happen again

- Reconciling/restoring a relationship

- Forgetting what happened

Forgiveness is also not something you do for someone else. In fact, you don't need anyone else (or even the request of anyone else) in order to forgive.

Forgiveness *is*:

- Accepting what happened, regardless of how painful it was

- Letting go of trying to change what already took place

- Releasing the resentment, anger, guilt, and shame

- Allowing yourself to learn from the past and make positive changes in your present and future

In other words, we are talking about forgiving what happened in the past and using it to your advantage. Forgiving—yourself, others, situations, a higher power—is vital to failing forward. Use what happened as data to move on and improve your life. Replace your fear of repeating a failure with forgiveness.

When old thought patterns come up that bring resentment or shame, try instead to focus on the following:

- ✓ "I can't change the past but I can change the present and future."

- ✓ "I choose to learn from the experience."

- ✓ "Although that experience was difficult, I did gain something positive from it (perhaps friends, understanding, the ability to help others)."

- ✓ "I am stronger today because of that experience."

- ✓ "I am proud of myself for persevering."

- ✓ "I believe things happen for a reason, even if right now I don't know what that reason is."

EXERCISE: GAINING FROM YOUR DATA AND FORGIVING

Think back on an incident that didn't go well. Then complete the sentences to follow.

Although that experience was difficult, I did gain something positive from it. I gained . . .

_____

_____

_____

_____

Next time something like that happens, I will . . .

_____

_____

_____

If you struggle with forgiveness, write out what your life would be like if your heart was full of forgiveness—think acceptance, perseverance—rather than fear and anger.

_____

_____

_____

_____

_____

_____

_____

Note that when we forgive, we improve our:

✓ Emotional well-being

✓ Physical health

✓ Relationships

✓ Work

✓ Finances

✓ Fun

✓ Spirituality

Keep these benefits in mind as you work through forgiveness and fail forward.

BTP TIP: Stop Drinking That Poison

While some say that forgiveness is for the weak, it actually can require much strength. It's much easier to carry a grudge than to work through the process of forgiveness.

And do you know who is most affected by your lack of forgiveness? You! It's been said that not forgiving is like drinking poison and expecting the other person to die.

Who else is affected by your lack of forgiveness? The people you love and others around you.

If you think they're not affected, please stop kidding yourself. While the effect might not be ever present, your resentment (and/or shame) can impact your ability to love, to live a life of passion, and to be the authentic you.

Step 3: Identify Your Values

Rather than fixating on your fear of failure, always trying to minimize its likelihood, what if you focused instead on what you want in life? When your attention is directed toward reducing the negative, there's a tendency to feel more fear and anxiety, more overall stress. In contrast, focusing on increasing the positive—striving for something you want—can help you feel more motivated and fulfilled.

One way to focus on what you want is to integrate your values into your everyday life. Values are characteristics that are considered intrinsically desirable and positive. When we live by our values—when we dedicate time and effort to what's important to us—we feel happier, more positive, more confident, and more empowered. It is as if we are saying, "Ah, this is what I am supposed to be doing."

> **BTP TIP: Do a Values Check**
>
> Look at your values. Then look at how you spend your time. Do the two categories add up? For many of us, how we spend our time does not reflect our values. For example, you may highly value fun, but that may not always be reflected in the time end energy you put into truly enjoying yourself. Balancing your time and values will help you live a Better Than Perfect life.

Perhaps you're unclear about what your personal values are. There are several ways to figure out your value system. One is to do the following exercise.

EXERCISE: IDENTIFY YOUR VALUES

Identify someone you look up to: a role model, mentor, hero, or heroine. This person may be alive or no longer on this earth. He or she may be real, fictional, a famous figure, or a person in your life.

_____

Now list the three qualities you most admire about this person:

_____

_____

_____

Turns out, these are three qualities that you value most in yourself and your life. Now that we've identified them, let's learn how to integrate these values into your life.

> Gary started seeing me after he received some complaints from his employees. Gary got the job done, no doubt about it, but, as his team described, "He makes us miserable in the process."
>
> Gary was both an asset and a liability to his company. Though he produced the highest revenues, his managerial methods also incurred the highest turnover rate. His bosses were tired of the effort and expense of replacing the string of employees who couldn't work with him.
>
> "I have to push them hard," Gary said about his staff. "We have to get good results. We cannot fail. Failure is not an option."

Working with the values exercise, Gary identified the following:

PERSON I ADMIRE: legendary UCLA basketball coach John Wooden

Top three qualities I admire about this person:

• He led by example. I admire his leadership.

• He continued to learn, despite being so successful. I admire his love of learning.

• He never gave up. I admire his perseverance.

Next, Gary identified five ways he could apply each value in his own life.

CHARACTERISTIC: LEADERSHIP

1. Have lunch with one staff member each week, asking for input about how to improve our team.

2. Elicit feedback annually.

3. Hold quarterly town meetings.

4. Before asking someone to do something, ask myself, "Would I do this myself?"

5. Openly express my appreciation for everyone's hard work.

Once Gary started applying these concepts in his work life, he learned a great deal. He truly listened to what his staff had to say rather than just telling them what to do. With this better understanding of his staff's strengths, he was able to leverage them to greater benefit for all.

Ultimately, when Gary focused on what he wanted (to be a great leader), rather than on what he didn't want (failure), he found that his stress levels reduced—and so did the stress of the people he led. As a result, Gary's division enjoyed a 12 percent increase in profits—without the previous turnover.

As you can see, Gary's effective use of this technique resulted in benefits not only to him, but to those around him as well.

EXERCISE: INTEGRATING YOUR VALUES

Now it's your turn. For each of the three qualities you identified in the person you admire, write out five ways to apply that characteristic in your own life.

CHARACTERISTIC:

1. _____

_____

2. _____

_____

3. _____

_____

4. _____

_____

5. _____

_____

CHARACTERISTIC:

1.

_____

2.

_____

3.

_____

4.

_____

5.

CHARACTERISTIC:

1.

_____

2.

_____

3.

_____

4.

_____

5.

_____

"Be more concerned with your character than your reputation, because your character is what you really are, while your reputation is merely what others think you are."
—JOHN WOODEN

You can find a values assessment form to help you figure out your unique value system at www.ElizabethLombardo.com/Better ThanPerfect.

CHAPTER 9

E: Eliminate Extremes

"Everything in moderation, including moderation."
—OSCAR WILDE

PERFECTIONIST THINKING IS based on extremes, such as viewing people, events, or circumstances in an all-or-nothing fashion. This component of perfectionism is shared by so many of us that we don't even realize how influential extreme thinking is. One of the best examples of this type of thinking comes every year on January 1.

> *"I'm giving up all chocolate, chips, and dessert. No more fast food. No alcohol. And I'm going to start going to the gym every day."*
>
> So Annie informed me the first time she called me to set up an appointment. It was December 22, and we were scheduling

our first session for right after the New Year. Like over 150 million Americans, Annie had set a New Year's resolution: to lose weight.

As we spoke, Annie shared that she had a history of losing and gaining weight. "I have done pretty much every diet out there—the nonfat diet, the 'no eating after 6:00 pm diet,' the 'cookie' diet where I ate these things that looked like cookies but tasted like crap. One time I ate only frozen dinners for three weeks, but was so hungry I had to stop.

"I once lost over thirty-five pounds by not eating any carbs. I gained it all back, though, and then some. . . . Maybe I should try giving up all carbs again?"

Here was a twenty-nine-year-old woman who desperately wanted to lose weight and keep it off, but her past was haunting her.

Fast forward to our first session: January 5. There were snow flurries dancing outside as Annie and I sat down together.

"I am just so pathetic. I have no willpower," she said. "This will never work. I should have just canceled my appointment today. I am completely hopeless."

I asked Annie what was going on. "I went to a brunch on New Year's Day. New Year's Day! Here I was, all excited to not eat anything. I was going to be good. This was the new me, after all.

"But what happened? I gave in. I broke down. I failed."

She went on to explain, "I was good for the first hour or so. Everyone else was shoveling food in their mouths. Oh, it looked so good. I kept thinking, 'This is so unfair. I wish I could eat that pastry and that bacon and everything else.' I was so hungry.

"Then I just gave in. I grabbed a cinnamon roll and practically shoved it down my throat. After that, it was all over. I started eating everything in sight. Later, I almost threw up I was so full. I'm never going to lose weight!"

When I asked how her exercise was coming along, she looked at me like I was crazy. "I already failed the diet. Why would I exercise?"

Can you relate to Annie's extremes? Have you ever thought:

- "I already ate one thing I wasn't 'supposed' to, so I might as well keep eating."

- "I missed a workout this week, so I'll just wait until next week to start again."

- "I failed in the past, so why bother trying again."

- "I can never do that."

- "I always mess up."

- "Things will never really change."

Layers of Extremes

Perfectionists think in extremes:

- All or nothing

- Black or white

- Perfection or failure

This extreme thinking has two layers:

- Extreme thinking about an event: "What I (or others) do is either perfect or a failure."

- Personalizing failure: "If what I do is a failure, then *I* am a failure."

This second layer of perfectionism is powerful, and one that is not often talked about. In fact, it's one reason why people have such difficulty releasing their perfectionism. Addressing the first layer but not the second will keep you in the familiar constraints of perfectionism, and will prevent you from living a Better Than Perfect life.

Since it's so important not to overlook personalization, we're going to discuss it first.

"The fastest way to break the cycle of perfectionism and become a fearless mother is to give up the idea of doing it perfectly—indeed to embrace uncertainty and imperfection."

—Arianna Huffington

Personalizing Failure

When you tell a perfectionist, "Relax, it doesn't have to be perfect," rationally she knows that's true. And yet on a deeper level she's thinking, "If it's not perfect, then it's a failure. And if it's a failure, then I'm a failure. So, essentially you're saying it's okay for me to be a failure." And that belief does not jibe with anyone.

It is this personalization that drives perfectionists, and it's why they can react in such extreme ways when they don't reach their goal. It's a matter of self-esteem.

According to psychologist Abraham Maslow's Hierarchy of Needs, esteem is a human need. Esteem includes the desire to be accepted and valued by others. And perfectionists often base their self-esteem on both what they do and how others react to what they do.

A good example of this is what I call New Mommy Syndrome. I'm referring to the state of attempted perfection that many new mothers adopt when they first bring their child home from the hospital. I know I sure did.

> *Twelve days before my due date, eleven hours after my husband and I arrived at the hospital, a beautiful baby arrived.*
>
> *She was bald and tiny, twenty-one inches long, and weighed five pounds, six ounces. Her fingers were so long, I was convinced she'd be a piano player like her great-grandmother.*
>
> *As I held this miniature being in my arms, staring down in wonder that she had come out of me, I vowed to take care of her forever, to love her unconditionally, and to be a perfect mother.*

Before she arrived, I had read what seemed like every book there was about parenting. I knew how vital breast-feeding was, what kind of visual stimulation was optimal at what age, and the importance of developing a predictable schedule of sleeping, eating, and playing.

Now that she was home, I resolved to apply every concept I had learned. After all, I've promised her I will be perfect.

And so my New Mommy Syndrome began. I was determined to do everything "right." Little did I realize the cost.

Afraid that she would suffer from Sudden Infant Death Syndrome, I watched over my daughter day and night. The consequence? No sleep for me.

If my husband tried to change her diaper, I monitored his every move, offering (unsolicited) feedback.

I declined friends' offers of help. I thought a perfect mom did it all on her own.

And then there was breast-feeding. I was determined my child would be exclusively breast-fed. No matter how much stress it caused me (a lot), no matter how hard it was on me, she would drink only breast milk. I spent hours each day trying to get her to eat more, and ended up hiring lactation specialists to help me. (I had no idea back then that my drive to be perfect probably dried up my milk.)

My daughter had colic, which meant that she cried for about eighteen hours a day for the first three months. She cried and screamed and cried.

When my sister came to visit, she told my husband, "I thought you were exaggerating about her crying. I mean, babies cry. But I have never seen anything like this."

Though my sister's comment made me feel a bit better, in my mind I was a complete failure as a mom. My baby cried all the time. I could not get her to eat. I had not slept in weeks. This was nothing like what I thought it would be.

While the books I read offered important ideas, my baby had not read these books. I needed to apply what actually worked for my family and me—and I needed to figure out what those things were.

The first time I "gave in" and tried bottle feeding, my daughter slept five hours straight—longer than she ever had before.

When I let her cry a little when she woke up, rather than rushing to her side as I'd previously done, I noticed that she actually soothed herself back to sleep.

When I let a babysitter come in and help us out—and even let her watch the baby so my husband and I could go out to dinner—I realized that sometimes part of being a good parent is accepting the help of others.

Have you ever experienced New Mommy Syndrome? Being a good mom means taking care of your psychological and physical well-being, as well as those of your child.

Have there been times in your life when you so desperately wanted something to be perfect that you gave it all your time, energy, and effort, only to have things not go your way?

> **BTP TIP: Mom, Take Care of Yourself**
> A happy and healthy mom translates into a happier and healthier baby. If you're a new mom, make sure you are taking care of you—if not for you, then for your baby. If friends whom you trust offer to help, let them.
>
> Make sure you get some exercise. Walking outside with your baby is great. So is going to an exercise class or getting on a cardio machine and catching up on your favorite TV show. And spend one-on-one time with your husband. He was used to being your true love and may now feel less important. Enjoy couple time together, even if it's in shorter spurts than before. A happy and healthy family makes for a happier and healthier baby!

To follow we'll discuss three situations that can elicit extreme thinking:

- Mind Reading

- Minimizing Achievement

- Labeling

I Can Read Your Mind

As mentioned earlier, we are mind reading when we *assume* what other people think without actually *knowing* what they think.

Consider this:

The tears in Lilly's eyes flowed down her cheeks.

"I am never going to find someone. I'm a complete loser. I'm going to grow old alone. I'll be dead for days and no one will even know it."

Lilly's boyfriend of six months had ended their relationship the evening before, saying he needed to focus on work instead.

"What he really was saying was I'm not worth his time. I am completely worthless," Lilly declared.

In Lilly's extreme thinking, she looked something like this:

EITHER...	OR
In a relationship	Lonely forever
Someone else cares about me	No one cares about me
Worthy of love	Completely unlovable

Consider times you may have assumed you knew what others thought or felt, even if they hadn't told you. How many times have you said, "I *know* he thinks . . ."? Lots of times we don't even include the "I know" in that statement; it's just "She thinks I am . . ." We can convince ourselves this statement is an absolute truth, letting our inner critic drive our thoughts. Extreme and inaccurate thinking can leave us feeling lousy.

It's Not That Big of a Deal

In addition to personalizing "failure" and mind reading, perfectionists often minimize their achievements. They rarely give themselves credit—or at least not for too long. So, rather than rating themselves on the "I'm perfect versus I'm a failure" scale, they rate themselves on the "I'm okay versus I'm a failure" scale. And their criteria for "okay" are their high standards. But even when they do achieve their high standards, perfectionists rarely say, "Wow, I did that perfectly." Instead they think, "It was okay. Now I need to focus on my next goal," with minimal time spent reflecting on what already has been achieved.

> *Remember Annie, at the beginning of the chapter, who wanted to lose weight? About two months into our working together, she informed me she'd dropped fifteen pounds.*
>
> *"Wow," I said. "That's really terrific."*
>
> *"Yeah," she replied. "But I still have at least twenty-five more to go. I'm not even halfway there . . ."*

Can you relate? Do any of the items below sound familiar to you?

- Are there times when, after an achievement, you're happy temporarily, but then turn your focus on the next goal, discounting your success?

- When someone congratulates you on a success, do you try to change the subject?

- When someone says, "Wow, great job!" do you answer, "Yeah, but . . ."? As in, "Yeah, but I still have so much more to do"? Or, "Yeah, but it wasn't that hard; anyone could have done it"?

- Are you uncomfortable when others celebrate your successes?

Why do perfectionists do this? There are two main reasons. First, we do not want to celebrate something until it's complete—perfectly done. Extreme thinking makes it feel inappropriate to applaud something that's unfinished. Second, we don't like to "brag." Extreme-thinking perfectionists often think, "If I let people make a big deal over what I've done, then I'll be seen as a show-off. I don't want people to think I'm boasting."

BTP TIP: Say Thank You

Feeling proud of your accomplishments is not the same thing as bragging. We're often taught it's impolite to brag—young females especially hear this. As a result, many of us generalize this to mean it's impolite to feel good about what you've done or to let others know you feel good.

Incessantly talking about how great you are is certainly not desirable. Let's face it, though, that's not an extreme we're discussing here.

So the next time someone compliments or congratulates you, rather than refute them, simply say, "Thank you." Allow yourself to experience gratitude for their kind words—as well as for what you've accomplished.

Gratitude is an important ingredient in a Better Than Perfect life.

What if you changed your extreme thinking to stop minimizing your achievements? Is it possible to be proud of what you have done, even if there is still more you'd like to do?

Say a friend wanted to become a medical doctor. When she received her bachelor's degree, would you say, "Yeah, but you still have to go to medical school"?

No way. You would celebrate with her and encourage her to keep up the same incredible work she had been doing.

So, then, what if you did the same for yourself? And what would it be like if you could actually appreciate and feel proud of yourself for what you've done—without being boastful? I bet it would feel pretty good!

Labeling

Labels can be extreme ways to see others. Do any of these sound familiar?

+ "Oh, she's a worrywart."

+ "He's lazy."

+ "My job is miserable."

+ "My brother is selfish."

+ "My coworker doesn't like me."

+ "I'm a failure."

Even the word "perfectionist" is a label. When writing this book, I really struggled with using this term, because I did not want readers to pigeonhole themselves as perfectionists. Why? When we use labels to describe someone, that label becomes a lens through which we see them—or ourselves.

"I don't like labels. I don't understand the need for them. When you define yourself a certain way, people have expectations."
—EDDIE HUANG

You might be thinking, "Yeah, but my labels are accurate. They're from past experiences with these people." While it may be true that this label categorized their past actions, continuing to use this label can influence how we interact with them now and in the future—and consequently how they interact with us.

Consider the following scenarios viewed through the lenses of different labels.

EVENT: Husband comes home from work, changes into comfy clothes after saying hello, then sits on the couch with his feet on the table.

LABEL 1: "My husband is so loving—he works hard to help support us."

- *Thoughts.* "He's relaxing after a long day at work."

- *Behaviors.* Smile, give him a kiss, ask him about his day—maybe even sit with him for a minute or two. This makes him feel appreciated. Later, after dinner, he tells you to sit down while he cleans up.

LABEL 2: "My husband is lazy."

- *Thoughts.* "Seriously?! Must be nice to sit down while some of us are still working."

- *Behaviors.* Passive-aggressive comments, not wanting to spend time with him. This causes him to avoid you—as well as the dishes after dinner.

"Labels are for filing. Labels are for clothing. Labels are not for people."

—MARTINA NAVRATILOVA

EVENT: There's a new hire at work being touted as a superstar in your field. On her first day, she is quiet and a bit reserved.

LABEL 1: "She is shy."

- *Thoughts.* "It must be tough entering a new office where you don't know anyone."

- *Behaviors.* You introduce yourself and ask if she'd like to join you for lunch. You realize that she is indeed shy—and also a really interesting person.

LABEL 2: "She is stuck up."

- *Thoughts.* "She won't even have a conversation with us."

- *Behaviors.* Avoid her. Talk about her behind her back. That she continues to stay away from you "proves" you were right about her.

Labels are extreme lenses through which you see others. They influence your feelings, thoughts, and actions toward a person; your feelings, thoughts, and actions in turn influence that person's responses to you.

But labels don't just distort your view of others. The labels you have for yourself can be equally as harmful.

EVENT: You apply for a position you want: a new job, a new company, a volunteer opportunity, a class. They decline.

LABEL 1: "I'm still successful."

- *Thoughts.* "I'll just find another position that looks interesting."

- *Behaviors.* Talk with others about various opportunities, find another, maybe even better position, apply for it, and get accepted.

LABEL 2: "I'm stuck in my pathetic life."

- *Thoughts.* "I knew I shouldn't have even bothered. This is my life; I just have to live with it."

- *Behaviors.* Don't try again. Sulk, feeling hopeless.

Be wary of the extreme negative labels you have for yourself and others.

BTP TIP: Try on Different Labels

Challenge the labels you've given the people in your life, and experiment with new ones.

For example, if you previously viewed a coworker, neighbor, or family member as "grumpy," how would your reaction to her differ if, instead, you viewed her as stressed-out or depressed?

Using the Over-Under Principle we talked about in Chapter 4: "Fear Versus Passion," find a new way to see people in your life—including yourself—that is less judgmental and more empathetic. See how your perspective, thoughts, behaviors, and feelings can change, simply by switching how you classify yourself and others.

WHAT AM I WORTH?

In this chapter we've been considering how people with perfectionist tendencies often view their world in extremes: personalizing failure, mind reading, minimizing their achievements, and labeling themselves and others. Why do they do this? Answer: conditional self-worth.

Perfectionists have a conditional sense of self. They base their view of themselves on external events—either what they do or how others react to what they do.

One place I see this is with parents who want to be their child's friend rather than their authoritative figure.

Sitting in the audience, I'm trying to look casual despite the fact that a huge video camera is pointing at me.

I look up and realize that Steve Harvey is introducing me.

"Hi, Doc," says Steve. "It's good to see you again. Should Pamela be shocked that her daughter is acting this way?"

We had been listening to Pamela's story of how her teenage daughter was going out until all hours of the morning, basically acting as if she could do whatever she wanted. Pamela had tried to get her daughter to abide by the rules, but she just "couldn't."

When questioned by Steve about how she approached her daughter, Pamela expressed a desire to be her daughter's friend.

My advice? "Be a parent, not a friend," I explained to Pamela and the viewers. "Yes, you want your children to like you. But you also want to give them a foundation for success, which includes morality, honesty, integrity, resilience, and purpose.

"Children need to know what the rules are and what the consequences will be if they are broken. Part of childhood is to test authority. An important part of parenthood is to

establish and maintain the rules, which means to consistently invoke the established consequences of broken rules.

"Love your children unconditionally and be their parent. That is what they need," I finished.

And don't rely on how your child or others view you to determine your worth.

Can you relate? Do you use others' reactions as a barometer to determine how you feel about yourself?

EXERCISE: WHAT ARE YOU WORTH?

To figure this out, consider a time when you felt good about yourself. Describe what brought about those good feelings.

_____

_____

Now describe what has to happen in order for you to really love yourself.

_____

_____

What actions or accomplishments are necessary for you to love yourself?

_____

_____

What do others need to do for you so you love or feel good about yourself?

_____

_____

While many people's beliefs about themselves are influenced by personal external events, a perfectionist tends to go to extremes.

EXTREMES WITHIN PERFECTIONISM

Perfectionists not only think in extremes, they also represent extremes. Remember Annie at the beginning of the chapter—the woman whose extreme thinking led her to be overweight? Well, that same kind of extreme thinking can also land us at the other end of the weight spectrum.

> *Meredith's frame was so fragile I could imagine her breaking into two at any moment. Her collarbones practically popped out of her long-sleeved, kelly green shirt. Under her jeans, her legs looked like thin twigs.*
>
> *"My dad keeps nagging me about eating," she told me. "He's always on me about my weight."*
>
> *At five foot five, Meredith weighed 100 pounds. The healthy weight for a woman her height and frame is closer to 130–140 pounds. By most standards, this twenty-one-year-old was severely underweight.*
>
> *"What do you think about your weight?" I asked.*
>
> *"I think I could stand to lose a few pounds."*

Anorexia nervosa is characterized by extreme attempts to lose and keep off weight, for example excessive exercising and/or eating less than is healthy for your body. When it comes to treatment, though, an important insight about anorexia is that food is merely a symptom of an underlying issue.

People with anorexia use food to extremes: to gain control, to boost their self-worth, to be happy. The problem is, someone struggling with anorexia never sees herself as achieving a state of thinness. Her definition of "thin" keeps changing, becoming more and more stringent, dangerous, and extreme.

This is often a manifestation of a perfectionist's extreme thinking, such as:

- "If I'm not thin, then I'm fat."

- "If I am fat, I am a loser. If I am thin, I am okay."

Please know that anorexia is a very treatable disorder. With support and guidance, the anorexic person can find other ways to develop a sense of control, lessen her extreme thinking, feel more relaxed about food, and, ultimately, learn to love herself unconditionally.

"I always tell the truth. Even when I lie."
—AL PACINO IN *SCARFACE*

Extreme Words

Words can be very powerful. And extreme words cause us to think in extreme ways.

Consider how often you use the following words:

- Always

- Never (and its cousin, "never ever")

- Forever

- No one

- Everyone

- Nothing

- Only

- Complete (as in "complete failure")

- Total (as in "total loser")

These words are red flags. They are a warning saying, "Slow down—you're being extreme." Why? Because these words can cause unwanted stress and behaviors.

Consider what Annie, from the beginning of the chapter, said about herself: "I will never be able to keep off the weight. I will always be fat!"

This deep-seated belief in extremes will, ultimately, become true. When we have a belief about ourselves, it affects how we think, act, and feel. What you believe, you will eventually achieve—even if it's something you don't want.

I see a common theme among the clients who want healthier bodies: if they don't change the way they view themselves, their bodies will not maintain any changes they achieve. The words we use can affect our actions, even without our realizing it.

One of the goals of the Better Than Perfect program is to help you cultivate thinking that is (1) realistic, and (2) helpful.

What you believe, you will achieve.

Extreme thinking tends to be inaccurate. There are very few real extremes in life, partly because we're human. I mean, "good" people can sometimes do bad things, and "bad" people can sometimes do good things. Positive relationships can have their unpleasant moments, and unhealthy relationships likely have had a few pleasant moments. And we've seen how too much or too little food/exercise can be unhealthy. Even characteristics in our partners are not all or nothing.

BTP TIP: Being Happy Attracts Great Partners

The happier you are, the more likely you are to attract someone who is also positive, someone who's a good match for you. If you're single and want to be in a relationship, in addition to putting yourself out there, take steps to address your own happiness and health. Exercise, take a fun class, volunteer, eat healthy foods, get enough sleep; all of these will help your physical and psychological well-being. The bonus: doing these things will raise your level of energy. And, since like energies attract like energies, you are more likely to meet someone who is as positive as you are.

In my practice, I often work with couples who are unhappy in their marriages. All-or-nothing complaints often fly in the first session. "He's always so lazy." Or, "She's ridiculously uptight." They conclude, "We will never be happy."

One of the first assignments I ask couples to do is to identify what each one found attractive in the other at the beginning of their relationship. The comments I often hear include "He was so laid-back," and "She was so energetic, always up for doing something fun." And what I often find is that the very attributes that attracted the couples to each other are the same characteristics they're criticizing in therapy, just less extreme versions.

The following is a sample of qualities that first attracted my clients to their partners, and which they now complain about.

SAMPLE: QUALITIES, IN EXTREMES

WHAT FIRST ATTRACTED SPOUSE	WHAT BOTHERS SPOUSE NOW
Laid-back	Completely lazy
Generous	Always squandering money
Spontaneous	Totally impulsive and irresponsible
Independent	Never wants to spend time with me
Caring	Completely overbearing
Thoughtful	Always obsessive
Organized	Totally uptight

Let me ask you, who wants to be with someone who is anal or impulsive and irresponsible? Not the characteristics of an ideal mate, right? But how about someone who is thoughtful or spontaneous? Certainly sounds more attractive!

> **BTP TIP: Take a Fresh Look at Your Significant Other**
>
> For those in a relationship, give this exercise a try. Name the qualities in your partner that you were first drawn to. Then look at how those same qualities are demonstrated today. How can you continue to embrace those characteristics? How would your relationship improve if you did?

You get to choose the words you use to describe your partner, your work, your life, and even yourself. Choose wisely to create a life you love.

MIGHT AS WELL GIVE UP

Thinking in extremes affects not only how we see ourselves and others. It also affects what we do. Not wanting to fail, perfectionists can give in to their extreme thoughts, and that often means giving up.

Have you found yourself thinking . . .

- "This is not working. It's never going to work. I give up."

- "This project is not going as planned. It's a complete waste of time. I'm going to ditch it."

- "My relationships always seem to start out great and then fall apart. So I'm getting out now."

- "She is always complaining about me; I'm not going to listen to anything she says."

- "My partner never helps around the house. I want out of this relationship."

- "No one understands me. Why bother talking to someone about this?"

The most extreme reaction to extreme thinking is the rapidly increasing rate of suicide in this country. About 12 people per 100,000 die by suicide every year. That works out to an annual rate of about 30,000 suicides. There are an additional 750,000 attempts at suicide.

BTP TIP: Just Ask! You Might Save a Life

I often hear people say they are nervous about asking someone they fear is suicidal if, in fact, he is thinking about killing himself. They worry that they might be planting the seed in the person's mind.

Research shows that's not the case. Someone in despair is not going to hurt himself just because you asked. He may, however, get the help he needs if you inquire.

What do you say? You might try something like, "I realize you've been feeling really upset lately. I want to help you in any way I can. I have to tell you, I am really concerned for you and your safety. Have you had thoughts about wanting to hurt yourself?" Then pause and wait for him to answer.

It is important that you convey empathy and love—with no judgment. Most likely, he is beating himself up enough. Your passing judgment on him will only add salt to the wound.

Also remember that someone who is suicidal is usually not thinking rationally. He is desperate.

People who are considering suicide are frequently ambivalent about whether to go through with it. They are often relieved to be able to talk about it with someone. You could be the person who offers that relief. Then get that person the professional help he needs immediately.

People don't choose to end their lives because of what is happening to them. People take such extreme measures because of their extreme thoughts.

Do you say any of the following statements to yourself?

- "It is never going to get better."

- "People will always make fun of me or talk about me behind my back."

- ◆ "No one really cares."

- ◆ "No one gets what I'm going through."

- ◆ "No one will really miss me."

- ◆ "I will always be a loser."

- ◆ "I can't do this anymore."

These extreme thoughts are based not on rational facts, but rather on overwhelming emotions. The problem is, people having these thoughts do not stop to really evaluate how true they are. Instead, they sink into a hole of hopelessness where the only option they see is to give up on life forever.

As I sit writing this book, there's another devastating suicide being reported in the media—this one at a prestigious college. A nineteen-year-old track star jumped to her death from a parking garage. Her father described his daughter as a "perfectionist" and attributed her death to the stress of college.

"At the end of high school and going to Penn, she was the happiest girl on the planet," he said.

Then things got tough for her. According to a family friend, "She got a 3.5 [grade point average] her first semester, and I think the high expectation that she put on herself was that those grades were just not acceptable."

Her interpretation of what "nonperfect" grades meant may have been a significant factor in why she ended her life. This decision has caused unimaginable pain for her family and friends—absolute devastation caused by extreme thinking.

If you are having thoughts about hurting yourself—or someone else—please seek help immediately. These extreme and mistaken thoughts could result in devastating actions for you and the people who love you. Realize that suicide is a permanent solution to a temporary problem.

ACTION STEPS: EMBRACE SHADES OF GRAY

Step 1: *Revise Extreme Thinking*

Step 2: *Try a Simple Start*

Step 3: *Reach Out to Someone*

Most of life is not black or white, but rather shades of gray. If those of us who tend toward extreme thinking start using language, applying behaviors, and viewing the world in a way that eliminates extremes, the result will be less stress, more confidence, and a Better Than Perfect life.

Step 1: Revise Extreme Thinking

Whenever you hear yourself say an extreme word, do three things:

1. Replace the all-or-nothing word with one that's not so extreme.

2. Identify at least three ways your original statement was not true.

3. Develop a new focus.

For example, Lilly, the woman we met earlier who was upset that her boyfriend had broken up with her, filled out the following form.

SAMPLE: REVISING EXTREME THINKING

REVISING EXTREME THINKING	
Extreme sentence:	No one is ever going to want to date me.
Extreme word used:	☐ Always ☐ Never ☑ No one ☐ Everyone ☐ Forever ☐ Nothing ☐ Only ☐ Other: _____
Revised statement:	I choose to focus on my happiness and be open to new people in my life.
Three piece of evidence to prove my extreme thinking is not accurate:	1. There have been other times when relationships ended, and new ones began later. 2. I have learned a lot from what didn't work in the past and can use those data to help me next time. 3. When I focus on coming from a place of love instead of fear, I've found that others are more attracted to me.
New focus:	I choose to focus on my happiness and be open to new people in my life.

EXERCISE: REVISING EXTREME THINKING

Now try it yourself. Think of something you have said or thought in the past week that was extreme. Then complete the form below.

REVISING EXTREME THINKING	
Extreme sentence:	
Extreme word used:	☐ Always ☐ Never ☐ No one ☐ Everyone ☐ Forever ☐ Nothing ☐ Only ☐ Other: _____
Revised statement:	

▶

Three pieces of evidence to prove my extreme thinking is not accurate:	1.
	2.
	3.
New focus:	

Use this form whenever any red flags of extreme thinking pop up for you—or for those around you.

Step 2: Try a Simple Start™

When we're feeling frustrated that we've not achieved our desired result, extreme thinking can make us give up early. Instead, set yourself up for success by setting short-term and long-term goals. And celebrate your achievements, even the smallest ones.

Consider this analogy. Let's say you want to get to the top of the Empire State Building by walking up its 1,576 stairs, a total of eighty-six floors. While you could wait until you get to the top to feel a sense of accomplishment, you could also pat yourself on the back for each floor you reach—or even for each step you take. Which would feel better? Which would be more motivating? And which would help you stay on track longer?

Even setbacks can be kept in perspective. Three steps forward and two back are still a net gain of one—plus you can learn from the two steps back.

Using a real-life example, let's go back to the situation Annie presented at the beginning of this chapter. Her all-or-nothing mentality is very common when it comes to weight loss and other health issues. I strongly believe that, if we can overcome extreme thinking, we can actually combat the health risks associated with eating disorders.

Almost 70 percent of Americans are overweight, and half of that number are obese. Obesity can lead to a host of problems, including diabetes, heart disease, stroke, sleep disorders, depression, and even early death. These health consequences also bring with them a huge financial cost. In 2005 in the U.S., health-care costs relating to obesity were estimated at $190 billion.

Effective weight loss isn't just about knowing what food to eat in what quantities. In order to produce significant and lasting results, we

also need to change our mind-set about eating. It is this mental component that most programs are lacking, and what, in my opinion, is the
cause of most setbacks.

I have a saying: "Change your brain to lose weight and maintain."

By replacing extreme thinking—and eating—I have helped my clients develop the healthy bodies they want and deserve.

In fact, I am so passionate about helping people banish all-or-nothing mentalities about weight loss that I recently partnered with Weight
Watchers to help spread this important message. For example, we
are encouraging people to take a Simple Start™ to changes in eating.
Rather than doing what Annie did, vowing to give up "all chocolate,
chips, and dessert," if you gradually balance out your diet, replacing
unhealthy foods with healthier foods, you can lose weight without feeling deprived.

You want a piece of chocolate? No problem—and no need to
beat yourself up for it. Enjoy and savor each bite. Then during the
rest of your day look for other food options that are packed with
nutritional value.

Change your brain to lose weight and maintain.

Now let's apply these concepts to your life. I'll start with an example from my own life to get us started.

I *love* what I do. And when I get caught up in a project, I tend to
completely immerse myself in it: my time, my energy, my thoughts. Of
course, I also *love* my family and want to spend time with them—and
to have them feel loved. In an effort to tone down my extreme focus on

work, I decided to develop a plan that would help me stay connected to the project and to my family. Here's what I did:

> **BTP TIP: Start Working Out Gradually, Too**
>
> Exercise is certainly an important ingredient in any successful weight loss plan. And the concept of starting simple can be applied here, too.
>
> For example, start with a ten-minute workout, then progressively add on.
>
> Research shows that you can also break up your exercise and get equal benefit. For example, we burn the same amount of calories in three ten-minute walks as we do in one thirty-minute walk. And every bit counts! Be Better Than Perfect when it comes to exercise: some activity is always better than none.
>
> You can go to www.ElizabethLombardo.com/BetterThanPerfect to learn what my personal favorite workouts, especially for when you don't have a lot of time.

SAMPLE: TRY A SIMPLE START

MY GOAL IS: SPEND MORE TIME BEING PRESENT WITH FAMILY.		
THE STEPS TO ACHIEVE THIS GOAL ARE . . .	WEEKLY CHECK-IN: I CHOOSE TO CHECK IN EVERY SUNDAY EVENING.	MY REACTION . . .
Stop work by 4:30 three afternoons each week to spend time with my daughters.	Did it twice. Was traveling this week.	Good to be there to help out with homework and hear about their days.
Daily spend at least twenty minutes of one-on-one time with each of my daughters.	Yes	Love to spend time reading with them at night.

▶

Spend at least thirty minutes of one-on-one time with my husband each day he is not traveling.	Yes	Enjoyed dinner two nights after the girls went to sleep.
Eat breakfast daily with my family when I am not traveling.	Yes	My oldest helped me make scrambled eggs one morning.
No checking cell phone or any other messages when I am doing any of the above.	Checked it twice. Otherwise, did it!	Not easy at first. Got easier as the week went on.

EXERCISE: TRY A SIMPLE START

Now it's your turn. Identify something you want to achieve. Can you break it down into the various steps necessary to complete it? Complete the table below.

MY GOAL IS:		
THE STEPS TO ACHIEVE THIS GOAL ARE...	WEEKLY CHECK-IN	MY REACTION...

▶

THE STEPS TO ACHIEVE THIS GOAL ARE . . .	WEEKLY CHECK-IN:	. MY REACTION . . .

Now, look at the first step in your table. What needs to happen in order for you to do this first step?

_____

_____

When will you complete this?

_____

How will you reward yourself when you do achieve this?

_____

_____

Now do it, and report back to us at www.facebook.com/Dr.Elizabeth .Lombardo. We want to celebrate with you!

Rewarding yourself for achieving your goal is very important—at each step. Allow yourself to feel gratitude for the changes that you made, the work that you did, and the difference you are making—one step at a time.

If your goal is to get to the top of the Empire State Building, there are lots of steps that need to be taken. Celebrate each and every step, while still keeping in mind your long-term goal of getting to the top.

BTP TIP: Kick Your "BUT"

Here's a secret to achieving any goal: make sure your "Why" (reasons for wanting this goal) outweighs your Buts (the obstacles that are present).

Staying focused on *why* you want to achieve this goal will help you stay on track. Focus on your reasons for doing what you are doing, rather than the obstacles, or what you're missing because of it. For example, if you're trying to drop some pounds, viewing the steps to your goal as depriving yourself will likely make you crave the very foods you're avoiding. But that's just another example of how easily our brains focus on the negative. If you instead focus on the benefits you will see in your waistline, health, energy, even being a role model for others, that positive focus can help you stick to and eventually succeed at your goal.

EXERCISE: WHY YOU WANT TO KICK BUT

Add to the following table a goal that's meaningful to you. Then, in each row include an obstacle that's keeping you from attaining that goal. Try to think of as many obstacles as you can. Finally, for each obstacle, include at least two benefits to sticking with your goal.

MY GOAL IS:		
ONE OBSTACLE TO REACHING MY GOAL IS . . .	ONE BENEFIT TO STICKING TO MY GOAL IS . . .	ANOTHER BENEFIT TO STICKING TO MY GOAL IS . . .

Step 3: Reach Out to Someone

Perfectionists regularly feel as if they need to do it all—and on their own. They often feel a strong tendency to isolate themselves psychologically from others; unfortunately this isolation makes them feel more alone and detached from others.

The fact is, we are social beings. And one of our intrinsic needs is to have social connections: to experience a sense of belonging, love, and acceptance. Trying to deal with the issues of life all alone can set you up for depression and loneliness. It also makes achieving your goal that much harder.

In my personal life, I was reluctant in the past to let people "in" on the various trials I went through. I'd developed the belief that I needed to be upbeat all the time so I could bring more joy to my friends; I also didn't want to be seen as a complainer. (Note how these are both examples of extreme thinking.) To my mind it was easier to keep bummer stuff in than to reach out for emotional and even tangible support from others. What's more, I was afraid to be vulnerable with others for fear of being hurt. I didn't want people to see the less than pleasant parts of me.

Can you relate?

Then I realized we are not perfect beings. We are Better Than Perfect. We can be vulnerable without going to extremes of being blubbery all the time. We can get help from loved ones while also supporting them. We can be honest about how things are going while still being a source of positivity and inspiration to those around us.

And it feels good to allow people in. One of the predominant themes I hear from my clients is "It feels so good to let this all out, to share this with someone, and to know that I am not alone."

So, whom can you reach out to? While I'm not necessarily suggesting you share with the world every single issue you struggle with (another example of extreme thinking), I have worked with clients who blogged about their struggles—and basked in the support they received.

But of course that approach doesn't work for everyone. How else could you get support from others?

- Reach out to someone you admire who can be a soundboard.

- Allow yourself to be vulnerable with a loved one.

- Have an accountability partner.

- Work with a coach or psychologist.

- Talk with a mentor.

EXERCISE: REACHING OUT TO SOMEONE

Right now, identify one person you will reach out to:

_____

_____

"There is no cosmetic beauty like happiness."
—MARIA MITCHELL

Take steps to eliminate extreme thinking to help you feel good about yourself, achieve the goals you want, and enjoy a life that is Better Than Perfect.

CHAPTER 10

C: Create, Don't Compare

"To live a creative life, we must lose our fear of being wrong."
—JOSEPH CHILTON PEARCE

IDEALLY, WE'D ALL be content with our lives, open to creating new possibilities. Unfortunately many perfectionists don't feel that way. Instead, in an attempt to feel good about themselves, perfectionists spend a lot of time comparing themselves and their accomplishments to others, defining and evaluating themselves based on how they stack up to those around them. This creates a sense of competition: me versus them. And in those comparisons perfectionists often judge themselves negatively. And, believe me, perfectionists do not like to lose.

While comparing themselves to others is not unique to perfectionists, they tend to be extremely intense in their comparisons. While this pressure may fuel their fire to work harder, that persistent inner critic can also cause a lot of stress, worry, anxiety, irritability, and insomnia, not to mention reduced productivity and creativity. In the balance, results are often less than favorable. Consider the following scenario.

"I'm always comparing myself to other people and feel like a loser," said Meg via Skype during our first coaching session.

When I asked her to say more about what she meant, Meg offered the following examples.

"When I go to a party and see what other people are wearing, I second-guess what I have on, even if I liked it before I went out.

"I see people at work and think, 'They are so put together. They probably never stress out like I do.' Then I beat myself up.

"Plus, I have FOMO (fear of missing out). When I'm trying to decide what to do on the weekend, I reach out to as many people as possible. I don't want to miss out on anything good. What if the man of my dreams is at a party that I miss? My friend Cathy never turns down a single invitation. I know she's going to get married before me."

"What is the experience of comparing like for you?" I asked her.

"Miserable. I have this voice screaming in my head: 'You suck. You are not good enough.'"

"So why do you do it?"

"Why? Because isn't that just part of life? I mean, how else will I know how I'm doing?"

"Good question," I said. "How else would you know how you're doing?"

*Meg was silent for a while. Then she said, "I don't know.
I mean, I guess I could look at other things, like how much
money I make or how many dates I have."*

*"Well," I responded, "how might you know how you're
doing without looking at external indicators?"*

*"You mean like how happy I am? But I only know how
happy I am if I compare myself to other people."*

"And how happy does that make you, in general?"

"Not very."

*"What if," I asked, "you could learn skills to help you be
happy without comparing yourself to others? What would
that be like for you?"*

*"I don't know if that's possible. Though it sure would be
great if it was," Meg added.*

*Luckily it is possible. And it was what Meg and I focused
on together.*

Can you relate to comparing yourself to others, and feeling as if
you fall short? Do you find yourself so focused on how you rate compared to others that you don't take the time to figure out what *you*
really want to create in *your* life?

ME VERSUS THEM

How often do you compare yourself with others using a mind-set of
me versus them? Has your desire to "prove" you are better ever prevented you from looking at what the best solution was for the problem
at hand?

By constantly comparing themselves with others, perfectionists develop a win-lose mentality: If I win, then they lose. If they win, then I lose. This results in feeling better about themselves (at least temporarily) when others "lose," even if it has nothing to do with them. There is a sense of "If I do better than he does, I'm okay. If he does better than I do, then I suck."

Do you ever wonder:

- "How is someone else better than I am?"

- "How am I better than someone else?"

- "What do I need to do in order to be better than that person?"

Perfectionists don't just want to "keep up with the Joneses," they want to kick the Joneses' butts!

Have you ever gone to a reunion and gloated over the fact that you looked better than others, or felt upset because others looked better than you? That's your inner critic talking.

This competitive edge is driven by low self-confidence. Trying to feel better about themselves, perfectionists use criteria from what others are doing to determine their own success and worth.

"At least Colleen didn't get the job either," Kristin said with a smirk on her face. This was in contrast to her usual scowl.

Kristin, an executive coaching client, had reached out to me after learning she'd been passed up for a promotion she'd worked hard for.

"I would have just died if she'd gotten it."

Kristin was referring to a colleague with whom she was secretly in competition. Although outwardly Kristin was kind to this woman, inside she had a "me versus her" mentality.

"Why is that?" I asked.

"Because if she had gotten it, I would have felt even worse about myself."

Perfectionists don't just want to "keep up with the Joneses," they want to kick the Joneses' butts!"

Can you relate? Do you ever:

- Feel better about yourself when others fail?

- Take pleasure in seeing others mess up?

- Secretly wish for others to flounder, especially those who you compare yourself to in some way?

The ever popular gossip columns and celebrity TV news shows encourage this superficial sense of competition. As a society, we love to see stars without makeup or with less than toned stomachs hanging out. People like to hear about who is cheating on whom, and are fascinated when celebrities make huge blunders.

Why? Because their "failure" becomes our gain.

When seeing a photo of a celeb without makeup (who has probably been Photoshopped to look even worse), we might think, "She looks *terrible*. Even I look better than that without makeup." It's as if someone else looking less than perfect makes us look better.

In reality, their looks have nothing to do with ours. We are independent entities. In fact, the world has the potential for limitless beauty, much like the potential for money, health, prosperity, and abundance. But perfectionists have a scarcity perspective: me versus them.

> *When I asked what Colleen's not getting the job had to do with Kristin progressing in her own career, Kristin was silent at first. Her head tilted a bit to her right as she glanced up, reflecting upon this question.*
>
> *"I guess it doesn't really. It just makes me feel better."*
> *"Why?"*
> *"Because if she didn't get it either, then I can't be that bad."*
> *"Who said you were bad?"*
> *"Me."*
> *"So you are comparing yourself with Colleen to determine how to view yourself?"*
> *Pause. "Yeah, I guess it is pretty pathetic, huh?"*

Feeling better about yourself when others don't succeed does not make you a bad person, so there's no need to judge yourself. Instead, you can make use of this key information now that it has revealed how you think and evaluate yourself. A perspective of "A failure for 'them' is a win for me" does not help you feel happier—not on a deeper, long-term level. It can, however, create negative energy—which can ultimately increase stress for you, and between you and others.

The research on envy—comparing what you have against what others have and perceiving that you fall short—offers important insights into the consequences of comparisons. For one thing, when you think others have it better, satisfaction with what you actually do have plummets. The "she has it better" thinking reduces your level of contentment, no matter how good you may have it.

Comparisons affect not only how we feel but also what we do to try to feel better. People will actually give up something positive in order to have someone else receive less. In one experiment, for example, participants were given the opportunity to get rid of other participants' money—though if they did they had to give up some of their own money, too. The result? More people chose to have others lose money, resulting in the depletion of their own funds. This indicates that the desire to feel better in comparison to others is stronger than any concern about the resulting cost. Of course, any boost in self-worth is superficial and temporary, so the gamble was a poor one.

This reaction of comparing yourself to others is not reserved for humans. Turns out brown capuchin monkeys will refuse an award if they see that other monkeys are getting a better one. Regardless of how common such comparisons are, they're not usually helpful to anyone.

THE PERFECTIONIST TREADMILL

In the world of positive psychology there is much discussion about the hedonic treadmill. This concept refers to the tendency to seek happiness via external pleasures. Once people have gotten that latest tech gadget or big vacation, they then look for the next pleasure. As a result, there is a constant striving for happiness with no permanent sense of contentment. There is a sense that "I will be happy when X happens," with X constantly changing once it's attained.

I find it's similar when it comes to perfectionism. But, rather than hedonistic rewards per se, what the perfectionist strives for is the next achievement, praise, or assets—before someone else gets them.

On a treadmill, when you take one step forward, that foot is ahead of the other. Quickly, though, that foot slides behind the other, causing the first foot to have to advance again. This process continues repeatedly as one foot tries, in essence, to one-up the other foot.

Here's an example of the perfectionistic treadmill I've experienced in my life:

- "I'll feel good about myself when I get my PhD."
  Done → Next

- "I'll feel good about myself when I get my psychology license."
  Done → Next

- "I'll feel good about myself when I have started my private practice."
  Done → Next

- "I'll feel good about myself when I write a book."
  Done → Next

- "I'll feel good about myself when my book becomes a bestseller."
  Done → Next

- "I'll feel good about myself when I get on TV."
  Done → Next

- "I'll feel good about myself when I get on *The Today Show*."
  Done → Next

Can you relate? (Stop comparing your perfectionist treadmill to mine!)

EXERCISE: REFLECTING ON THE PERFECTIONIST TREADMILL

Identify a time when you thought you'd feel good about yourself once some milestone was reached, only to replace that something with something else, yet another external experience you thought would bring you self-contentment.

_____

_____

_____

_____

_____

What would your life be like if you started to feel good about yourself right now?

_____

_____

_____

_____

"I think everybody should get rich and famous and do everything they ever dreamed of so they can see that it's not the answer."

—JIM CARREY

EXPERIENCE GRATITUDE

What if you got off the perfectionist treadmill? What if, instead of comparing yourself and your life to others, you felt a strong sense of gratitude? Gratitude refers to feeling appreciation and being thankful for the people, experiences, and tangible things in your life. It entails focusing more on what is going well than on what you think *should* be different.

"The struggle ends when gratitude begins."
—Neale Donald Walsch

A client once asked me, "If I feel grateful, won't that make me complacent and resigned to the way things are?" Absolutely not! Gratitude will not keep you from striving to be better. It will, however, help you stop comparing yourself to others, and allow you to feel good about who you are and what you have in your life.

Research shows that gratitude is a very powerful way to reduce anxiety, feel happier and more optimistic, be healthier, improve your relationships, and even do better at work. People who are grateful have more friends, are more liked—and are even perceived as being sexier.

Gratitude appears to stimulate certain areas of the brain that reduce stress, boost contentment, and increase feelings of self-worth, not to mention aiding in digestion and sleep. Imagine, all those benefits without popping a pill!

BTP TIP: Gratitude on the Job

Gratitude helps people be better managers, boosts productivity, and improves your ability to make decisions.

Sadly, 65 percent of Americans reported they didn't receive recognition at their workplace in the last year. Lack of appreciation is one of the top reasons people leave their jobs. As a result, neglecting to offer recognition can cost companies as much as 200 percent of an executive's salary.

The good news is that gratitude can be cultivated. In fact, when I conduct trainings on gratitude in the workplace, not only is there a healthier environment, but people express greater happiness, more energy, increased motivation, and better sales.

WHAT DO YOU THINK?

In addition to comparing themselves to others in terms of achievement, perfectionists compare or evaluate themselves according to others' reactions. They yearn for positive reactions from others. Examples of desired comments include:

- "Wow, I can't believe you stayed up all night to finish that."

- "It's crazy how hard you work."

- "You are by far our top performer."

- "Of course you won the award. There is no one better than you."

- "I wish I could do that."

Perfectionists can be rather needy when it comes to receiving external praise in order to feel good about themselves. They may minimize the recognition ("Oh, it's not that big of a deal"), but inside they thrive on what they view as positive feedback.

Sometimes this need creates tension within a relationship. More than once I've been upset with my husband for not being as happy as I thought he'd be about an achievement in my life. Inevitably, though, when I looked back at his reaction, he had, in fact, expressed his joy and delight. I was just "needing" more. In the past, this might have resulted in an argument. Now I try to be more in tune with his expressions. And if I want more, such as when I've spent three hours cleaning out closets for the family, I let him know.

BTP TIP: Listen to How Others Express Emotions

People express their emotions in different ways. Me, I'm a rather passionate person. When I'm happy, people around me know. When I'm excited for someone, I've been known to give her a cheer. (No, I was never a cheerleader—just a benchwarmer in field hockey—but I learned a cheer or two in my day!) I've even made up songs that I belt out to express my love to my daughters.

Others are more reserved in how they express their emotions. That doesn't mean they don't experience them—just that they communicate them in a different way.

Pay close attention to how the people in your life express emotions, so you can really hear and understand them.

Can you relate to relying on others' praise?

• How do other people's reactions affect how you view the significance of what you accomplish?

• Have you ever been upset that someone's reaction was not enthusiastic enough?

• Do you wait to hear how others react to you before you give yourself a pat on the back?

Certainly there's nothing wrong with wanting positive feedback from others. Issues can arise, though, when you allow others' reactions to determine your own internal and external reactions. Instead, try being your own cheerleader and best friend who loves you unconditionally and is proud of all that you do.

THE PERVERSE PRIDE OF COMPETITION

Perfectionists evaluate how they spend their time as a means of defining themselves. Output is equated with self-worth. This output includes both what is accomplished—the result—and simply the act of doing *something*. (For me, it's sometimes hard to sit down. I like to be "doing things.")

Somewhere along the way, perfectionists develop what I call the Perverse Pride of Competition (PPC): the competition for having a tougher situation than the next person as a way to feel better about themselves.

"Lunch is for wimps."
—MICHAEL DOUGLAS AS GORDON GECKO IN *WALL STREET*

Do any of these statements sound familiar?

- "I stayed up all night to work on this."

- "I haven't slept more than four hours in five years."

- "I haven't had a vacation in three years."

- "I never take all my vacation days."

- "I work fourteen-hour days."

- "My day starts at five in the morning and doesn't end until after midnight."

Don't get me wrong, though: perfectionists like to give off the image they have it all together—not a hair out of place or a project less than 100 percent. The point is to be seen as better than others.

Most of all, though, being busy is so important to perfectionists because they equate activity with worthiness. They have a mentality that says: "If I'm doing *something*, then I'm more significant. Doing nothing makes me a nothing."

Can you relate?

The underlying purpose of the Perverse Pride of Competition is to feel good about oneself. That's a basic human need, so this makes total sense. The concern is that busyness can often lead to other problems, such as:

- Decreased productivity

- Difficulty focusing

- Reduced efficiency

- Increased stress and anxiety

- Irritability

- Feeling overwhelmed

- Burnout

I'm sure you can relate to at least some of these. What happens to you when you're overly busy? What would life be like if, instead of feeling good about yourself because of your packed schedule, you felt good about yourself because you are you?

IT'S NOT YOU, IT'S ME

The comparisons we use to measure ourselves may not even be with a specific person, but rather regarding how we think we *should* be doing something. Let me show you an example.

> *I was sitting in a chair with my feet on the floor, hands in my lap, eyes closed. That's all I was doing. Not writing on my computer, checking my email, or speaking with a client. I was meditating.*
>
> *Or at least trying to.*
>
> *While getting my PhD, I had written articles about the benefits of meditation. I knew it was supposed to help boost*

your happiness, improve your health, reduce your stress, spur creativity, and enhance mental functioning.

It all sounded good. Until I tried to do it.

"Am I doing this right?" I'd ask myself. "Am I meditating? I don't think I'm in meditation, am I? I don't feel like I am meditating. Is it supposed to feel different?

"Ugh, wait, I'm not supposed to be thinking. My mind is supposed to be clear and free of thoughts. Okay, here we go.

"Darn, I'm hungry. What did I have for breakfast? Oh yeah, a yogurt. Well, no wonder I'm hungry. That was four hours ago.

"Did I remember to reply to Diana's email? I know she needs that information ASAP.

"Crap, I'm thinking again. I'm not supposed to think. I am supposed to be meditating.

"You know, twenty minutes is a long time. And I don't have a lot of time. If I stop meditating now, I could use this time to grab a snack and get back to Diana.

"No, I need to meditate. But it shouldn't be this hard. How hard could it be to just sit and not think? What is wrong with me?"

In comparing my meditation practice to what I thought I should be experiencing, I was not able to get the benefit of meditation. That comparison also caused me to stop trying altogether. Luckily, I later learned Transcendental Meditation (TM), which I highly recommend. During my training, my TM instructor, Peggy, told me, "There is no need to compare yourself to others, or even to other meditations you've had. Any meditation can be good. And your mind will wander sometimes. There is nothing wrong with that."

By stopping my comparisons and simply allowing myself to be present in the meditation, I am able to enjoy the benefits TM brings.

BTP TIP: Start Meditating

If you are not regularly practicing meditation, you have not fully realized the powerful impact meditation can have on your life. And here's an opportunity to practice Better Than Perfect living: *any* meditation is better than no meditation.

The Maharishi Foundation USA (www.tm.org) encourages people to spend twenty minutes twice a day in meditation.

That amount of time may feel overwhelming to you, so why not try just five minutes?

How do you meditate? There are lots of ways. You can sit quietly, focus on your breathing, repeat a mantra, listen to soothing music, look at nature, or listen to a recording of a meditation induction.

ANOTHER AREA I see people making comparisons is when they have medically unexplained symptoms (MUS): physical ailments that are not understood by conventional medical practices. In essence, some part of your body hurts, feels weird, or isn't working the way you want it to. Various types of chronic pain, fibromyalgia, chronic fatigue pain, noncardiac chest pain, and interstitial cystitis, among other conditions, fall into this category.

MUS can be extremely challenging. Not only are people dealing with distressing ailments, but their pain and suffering are amplified by their not being able to identify and treat what's ailing them. Often they go from doctor to doctor, desperate for help that's not forthcoming.

To make matters even more challenging, there is an underlying tension regarding the lack of medical "proof" that something is really going on. Our society tends to think that if something is wrong, we should go see a doctor. The doctor will diagnose you, and then will treat it if possible. If the doctor can't find anything wrong with you, then you must be making it up. People with MUS often worry that they'll be seen as hypochondriacs who fabricate symptoms just to get attention. The stress of trying to convince others that their symptoms are real just adds to the pain and suffering of the ailment itself.

In reality, the majority of symptoms people experience are medically unexplained. Research from the United States and the United Kingdom has demonstrated that three out of every four complaints made to primary care physicians are, in fact, medically unexplained. So, 75 percent of the time when someone says, "Doc, it hurts here," the doctor does not know why.

In my clinical practice, having worked with people with MUS for over a decade, I have found that a good portion of them are perfectionists.

> *It was with great reluctance that Lisa came to see me. For the past three years, she had been examined by over fifteen health-care providers trying to find help for her unexplained headaches.*
>
> *"I have seen neurologists, chiropractors, physical therapists, orthopedic surgeons, vascular surgeons, nutritionists. . . . You name it, I've seen them. And no one had a real clue of what's going on. I know this pain is real. I am not making it up. This is not supposed to feel this way."*

Lisa wanted me to know that her seeing me did not mean the pain was all in her head. I assured her, "I know what you are experiencing is very real. Just because we don't really understand why it's happening does not mean it is not happening. Chronic pain is stressful, and stress can make the pain worse. I help people reduce their stress, which helps decrease their pain."

Lisa seemed okay with that.

As we worked together, Lisa told me, "It's so unfair. No one else is dealing with this pain. No one else understands how hard it is. Everyone else has it so easy."

Without a doubt, pain can be debilitating to deal with. I would never minimize what someone is going through.

It is also important to realize that this type of unfair comparison leads to greater stress and often even more pain. Lisa was trying to convince others that what she was going through was not fair (and it definitely was not!). On the other hand, by focusing on her indignation, Lisa inadvertently prevented herself from reducing unneeded stress.

One of the first steps to treating medical unexplained symptoms is to accept that what you are feeling is "real" even if others don't get it. And, while it's not fair, these are the cards you've been dealt at this particular point. By taking the judgment and comparisons away, you are better able to take the steps you need to make positive changes in your life. In this manner, cognitive behavioral therapy has been shown in research studies to help people reduce their pain levels and increase their functional abilities.

Can you relate? Maybe you don't have medically unexplained ailments, but perhaps you've had experiences when you focus on the comparison between what is and what you think should be, and you feel "that is not fair." Rather than accepting where you are and then taking steps to make positive changes, holding on to this type of comparison actually prevents you from moving forward. Focus your energy not on trying to have the perfect life, but rather on a Better Than Perfect life. Then you can make progress toward having more happiness and health in your life.

If you suffer from any type of medically unexplained symptoms, applying the various principles and strategies in this book—which are based on cognitive behavioral therapy (CBT)—can be quite helpful. Research and my clinical experience show that CBT can help reduce pain and other physical symptoms, lessen distress and depression, boost confidence, improve sleep, improve your relationships, and help find passion and meaning in your life outside of your physical ailments.

HOBBIES? HUMBUG!

Perfectionists like to be good at . . . everything. If we can't be good at something, then we rationalize, "Why even bother doing it?"

Here's a little confession: I used to hate coloring with my daughters. Drawing is not one of my strengths, so I used to cringe when one of my children said, "Come draw with me, Mommy."

Why?

Because I judged my drawing. I was embarrassed when my daughter asked me to draw with her and then looked at my creation with confusion. I thought, "Obviously I suck at sketching, so why even try?!"

Because perfectionists base their self-worth on the outcome of what they do, they're selective about how they spend their time and judge themselves based on their activities. Many will put the majority of their time, energy, and effort into work. They may rationalize, "I have to do this in order for my business to be successful," or "I will get fired if I don't work this hard." And, while diligence is certainly important for professional success, perfectionists tend to work excessively. They work at the expense of leisure activities.

This can also be seen in the form of cleaning, organizing, or even decorating. Their home may be immaculate, every item having its own place.

Then there's the other end of the spectrum, where perfectionists will spend hours upon hours watching TV. With the mind-set of never being able to do something as well as someone else does, they are determined to watch every episode of the newest show, as well as the five seasons they missed before. While they can justify the time in front of a screen, they can't give themselves permission to do something else that is fun. A hobby is seen as frivolous and impractical. For some reason, though, TV gets the "okay."

In reality there are lots of benefits to having a hobby, regardless of how good you are. A hobby helps you be present, stimulates your mental powers, reduces stress, and even helps you be healthier. Regarding health, for example, research shows that doing something for fun can lower blood pressure, the stress hormone cortisol, and even your waist size!

And hobbies and other types of leisure activities can be especially wonderful pathways to creativity. Being passionate and excited about something you're engaged in creating is a surefire way to generate happiness in your life. That joy only increases and deepens with further involvement.

So, as your happiness coach, let me ask you: what activities are you not doing that you would love to do? Do you not do them because you keep comparing your abilities to others'? Any of the following?

- Dancing
- Singing
- Drawing or painting
- Sculpting or pottery
- Acting
- Cooking
- Playing a musical instrument
- Writing
- Inventing
- Learning a new language
- Knitting
- Model building
- Sewing
- Woodworking
- Yoga
- Photography
- Sports
- Exercising
- Reading

Stop comparing yourself with others and just go for it!

MAINTAINING FRIENDSHIPS

Sitting on the couch in my office, I was taking a few minutes out of my workday to chat with a friend who had called out of the blue. Though we'd been close in the past, we'd not spoken for over two years.

After we caught up on what had been going on in our lives, she told me, "I had what felt like a midlife crisis last week. I realized that, despite all the good stuff that's going on in my life with work and my family, I had completely lost touch with my friends."

Can you relate? Perfectionists tend to prioritize their work, health, family, and taking care of others. But time to just hang with friends is often reserved for "when I have time."

And in a perfectionist's hectic life, that time never seems to appear.

"I found out what the secret to life is—friends. Best friends."

—JESSICA TANDY IN *FRIED GREEN TOMATOES*

BTP TIP: Conquer Your Loneliness

Did you know you can be lonely despite having people around you? We feel lonely when we have a sense that people don't really care for or understand us on a deep level.

Sadly, there are serious consequences of loneliness, in addition to feeling sad and isolated. In fact, loneliness increases your chances of dying by 45 percent. To put this in perspective, obesity increases your chances of dying by 23 percent and excessive drinking increases your chances of dying by 37 percent.

If you feel lonely, you are not alone. At least one in five people—about sixty million Americans—suffers from loneliness.

What can you do? Be Better Than Perfect and start being more social. Meet new people by taking a fun class, joining a gym or Boot-Camp, joining a church, or volunteering. If you're shy with people, how about volunteering with animals?

Start to put yourself out there: speaking with others, asking people questions, sharing a bit about yourself. While you may be worried that people won't be interested in you, in my experience the majority of people are more concerned that you won't like them.

The benefits of friendship are countless. Research shows that friends are good for your health—whether we're talking stronger immune systems or less aggressive cancer or just plain living longer. Friends help reduce stress levels, help you get through difficult times, and help you feel connected. Self-confidence, happiness, resilience, and a sense of purpose all increase when you have close friends. Plus, they can bring us more fun, something that perfectionists often place low on their priority list despite wanting more of it.

As we get older, it can sometimes be harder to make or maintain friendships. You and others are busy. Maybe you've moved or changed jobs. Perhaps you're not spending time in the same circles as you used to.

Consider for a moment: what could you do to spend time with a friend—or try to make a new friend—this week?

☐ Schedule a lunch or dinner

☐ Meet at the gym

☐ Invite someone over

☐ Volunteer

☐ Go for a walk

☐ Participate in a networking or social group

☐ Invite a neighbor or colleague out for coffee

☐ Attend a community event

☐ Join a club or place of worship

☐ Take an interesting class

☐ Other: _____

ACTION STEPS: REDEFINE SUCCESS

Step 1: Build More Fun into Your Daily Life

Step 2: Be Your Own Best Friend

Step 3: Focus on Gratitude

Stop comparing and start living. Be the best, happiest, healthiest *you* possible without worrying about how you stack up against others or arbitrary standards.

Have you ever tried on a dress or pair of pants to find that the size you normally wear is too small? When this happens we can feel dread, frustration, and angst, assuming *we're* at fault, that we gained weight. But the fact is, different designers size their clothing differently: one's size 10 is another's size 12. By comparing the size 12 to the size 10 slacks we *think* we should fit into (independent of the true measurements), we feel like a failure. Let's stop that unnecessary self-judgment. Be comfortable—in your clothes and your skin. Try these tips to redefine your success.

Step 1: Build More Fun into Your Daily Life

How do you define *success*? If your definition of a successful life is focused solely on achieving X, Y, and Z, then you will constantly be comparing yourself to others, walking the perfectionist treadmill.

When you base your sense of success or worth on only one part of your life, you tend to put most of your time, energy, and effort into that facet, at the expense of family and friends and the other important things in your life.

For me, a life of happiness and meaning is the ultimate success. That includes important ingredients such as:

✓ Spending quality time with my daughters

✓ Spending quality time with my husband

✓ Spending quality time with friends

✓ Spending quality time with my parents and sister

✓ Doing something good for my community

✓ Exercising

✓ Meditating

✓ Continuing to grow in personal development

✓ Using my creative energy to produce a book or another project

✓ Getting good sleep

✓ Being a happiness coach (via coaching, speaking, writing, or TV appearances) and helping others be truly happy

✓ Having fun

✓ Laughing a lot

How about you? Write out your responses to the following questions.

EXERCISE: REDEFINING SUCCESS

How do you define *success*?

_____

_____

_____

What ingredients go into your success?

_____

_____

_____

_____

_____

_____

Now look again at your list. What "fun" did you include?

Ask yourself, "Would I rather be perfect or happy?" Most perfectionists would say "Happy," but think that, in order to do so, things need to be "perfect."

There are many approaches to increasing happiness. One is just to have more fun. It may sound a little elementary (are we talking about recess here?), but fun is not something that perfectionists tend to prioritize. I know I used to reserve fun for vacation (when I wasn't checking email or coaching a client—yes, I admit it).

So, here's a question you might not ask yourself every day: how can you have more fun? This doesn't mean I'm recommending you watch TV for hours, eating bonbons. I am suggesting that you look for ways to enjoy life a little more. No, *a lot more*.

This could include reading, learning something fun, working out, cooking, playing with your dog, chatting with a friend, or laughing at a funny show. It could also include applying your values and strengths as we discussed in Chapter 8: "Fail Forward."

There is no right or wrong answer. Just identify some things you'd like to do. I make sure I spend time snuggling and reading with my children every night, which is one of my favorite things to do. I take kickboxing classes, which give me a positive high. I take time-outs when I am working to watch a funny video with Ellen DeGeneres, Jon Stewart, or Jimmy Fallon.

EXERCISE: BUILDING MORE FUN INTO YOUR LIFE

What is one thing you will do today that will bring more fun into your life? Write it out here.

_____

_____

_____

_____

_____

And when you do it, share it with us at www.facebook.com/Dr.Elizabeth .Lombardo. We want to have fun hearing about your fun!

"My definition of success is to live your life in a way that causes you to feel a ton of pleasure and very little pain—and because of your lifestyle, have the people around you feel a lot more pleasure than they do pain."

—TONY ROBBINS

Step 2: Be Your Own Best Friend

If you could stick a microphone in your brain, what would you hear yourself saying about yourself? When working with perfectionists, I find they are often surprised at how downright mean they can be to themselves.

Do you ever say any of these things to yourself?

- "You suck!"

- "You are in *way* over your head."

- "Don't screw up . . ."

- "Did you *seriously* just say that?! They're going to think you are so stupid."

- "You are such a loser!"

The list could go on and on.

Face it, you would *never* say any of these things to a best friend—or even a stranger. So why say them to yourself? Instead, replace the negative judgments with statements of love, support, and empowerment.

This does not mean let yourself give up on your drive for excellence. If a friend said, "Eh, it doesn't matter how well I do on this project," you would probably not agree with her. You would, instead, offer words of encouragement and empathy to help her feel better about herself *and* take steps to produce excellence in her project.

To make this more concrete, the following are new ways to reframe fearful thoughts.

SAMPLE: REFRAMING YOUR FEARFUL THOUGHTS

RATHER THAN . . .	SAY THIS . . .
She is doing so much better than I am. I suck.	I am proud of myself for my progress and can continue to improve, learning from others.
I feel better because he screwed up.	I can empathize with how he feels.
I can only feel good about myself if others acknowledge my successes.	I choose to focus on applying my passions and values, which makes me feel good.
I need to be better.	I am grateful for the people, experiences, and things in my life.

EXERCISE: REFRAMING YOUR FEARFUL THOUGHTS

Now it's your turn. In the chart below, fill out the left column with things you say to yourself that make you feel lousy. Then, in the right column, reframe your self-talk to instead provoke passion and empowerment. If you have trouble, imagine what you would say to a loved one in the same situation.

RATHER THAN...	SAY THIS...

Step 3: Focus on Gratitude

Gratitude is about appreciating and being thankful. Gratitude is one of the fastest ways to be truly happy, and one of the longest-lasting ways to remain happy. Being grateful also helps reduce stress, improve relationships, enhance creativity, and boost health.

Given perfectionists' focus on preventing failure, they rarely take time out to concentrate on what they're grateful for. Some express concern that if they allow themselves to focus on gratitude they'll become complacent in other parts of their lives, which could lead to failure. This, however, is not true. Enjoying what you have does not prevent you from striving to keep making things better. In fact, the more gratitude you experience, the more people and experiences will come into your life that warrant gratitude.

I once gave a radio interview about how to be happier. During it a caller asked, "How can you be truly grateful for what you have while still striving to make things better?" This excellent question warrants explanation.

When we feel grateful, we appreciate what is happening in our life—the people, experiences, and situations we encounter. We are not judging it, considering how "things should be better." We are simply thankful for what we have. This doesn't stop us from planning to make things even better—say, with our health, relationships, or financial situation. We don't have to tell ourselves, "It will only be good when these changes happen." It's ultimately more helpful and more productive to think, "Things are good now, and they can continue to be good, even great."

This spirit of continuous improvement allows us to progress and still be grateful for what we have now.

Writer William Arthur Ward once said, "Feeling gratitude and not expressing it is like wrapping a present and not giving it." I say, "Not experiencing gratitude is like not opening the wrapped gifts surrounding you." Just as Christmas morning is a time for children to open their presents, every morning—and throughout the day—can be a time when we experience gratitude for our gifts: what we currently have in our lives.

EXERCISE: FOCUSING ON GRATITUDE

So, try this: every day, write out at least three things, people, or experiences that you appreciate. They can be absolutely anything that comes to mind—there are no right or wrong answers.

TODAY I AM GRATEFUL FOR...

1. _____

_____

_____

2. _____

_____

_____

3. _____

_____

_____

This can be challenging for some, especially those who have been so focused on "what's next" or "what needs to be better" rather than "what's already good." The fact is, you can start anywhere, appreciating even the small, even the seemingly mundane, things in life.

In my book *A Happy You: Your Ultimate Prescription for Happiness,* I posed the following question: "If you lost it all tomorrow, what would you miss most about today?" Now, I'm sure you can think of three things that you'd miss if you didn't have them; even, say, toilet paper. I mean, you probably don't have overwhelming feelings of gratitude when you reach for some toilet paper, but I bet you would sure miss it if it weren't there. So, yes, be grateful for even the toilet paper.

As you write down your three gratitudes, allow yourself to really feel your appreciation for them. One of the purposes of this exercise is to strengthen your gratitude muscle by identifying what you appreciate. The other is to help counter your fear and anxiety about failing, and reduce stress and anxiety. In short, gratitude is a powerful way to reduce your fears, have more joy in the present, and set yourself up for greater success in the future.

When is the best time to do this? That's up to you. Some clients like to write out what they're grateful for first thing in the morning to help set the stage for a joyous day. Others prefer doing it in the evening as a positive review of their day and a way to de-stress before bed. There is no "right" way, so see what works for you.

Also, be sure to periodically review your gratitude list—while feeling the appreciation for the items you identified. This is also a great way to reduce stress and fears. So keep this list in a place where you can readily access it—and even add to it!

BTP TIP: Use Gratitude to Change Your Perspective

If there is one area of your life that consistently causes you stress, use gratitude to help counter your perspective. Are you upset with your partner? Does your work feel overwhelming? Are you anxious about your kids? Is your body not looking or functioning the way you desire? Wherever you frequently experience stress, make sure you include a daily gratitude about that area of your life.

For example, one of the most powerful ways to relieve tension in a relationship is to focus on what you are grateful for in the other person. When we are at odds with others, we tend to be really good at identifying all the ways they messed up, all the things they do that annoy us. Focusing on gratitude rather than complaints, though, helps us see others more clearly for the wonderful people they are, even with their "faults."

Identifying the attributes you appreciate about a person or situation will help you change your perspective, which can reduce your stress and allow more joy. Gratitude is an important ingredient in living a Better Than Perfect life.

CHAPTER 11

T: Transcend

THE TERM "TRANSCEND" means to rise above ordinary limits, triumph over negativity, and go beyond. And that is exactly what being Better Than Perfect means: rising above the old ways we have limited ourselves with perfectionism, triumphing over our negative inner critic, and going beyond to a place of love rather than judgment.

Patty Stonesifer is an incredible example of transcending.

What do you do when money is not an issue for you? Sip iced beverages on the beach while someone fans you? Sleep until noon each day? Spend your afternoons lounging around?

Not Patty Stonesifer.

Her résumé is beyond impressive: she was the highest-ranked and highest-paid woman at Microsoft; assisted Bill and Melinda Gates in starting the Gates Foundation, where she oversaw a $39 billion endowment; and served as the chair of both the White House Council for Community Solutions *and the Smithsonian Institution's Board of Regents. She currently sits on the board of Amazon.com, Inc.*

Not surprisingly, given this history, Stonesifer is worth millions. And millions. Of dollars. She could do whatever she wanted with her life. And yet she chooses to work long hours in some of the least desirable areas in Washington, DC.

In April 2013, Patty Stonesifer became the head of Martha's Table, a food pantry and family-services nonprofit organization with a budget of about $6 million. Her days are long, starting in the wee hours of the morning and ending often late at night. According to Forbes, she spends a third of her time working on broad issues related to child hunger both in DC and nationally; another third on a strategic plan for the future of Martha's Table; and a third interacting with staffers, volunteers, and clients.

As The Washington Post *noted, "Having Stonesifer come run a small local charity is like General Electric business titan Jack Welch showing up to manage the corner appliance store."*

And yet that is exactly the place she chose to devote her time, energy, and passion. As she has said, "This idea that the District has so much child hunger, it's mind-boggling."

Stonesifer transcended stereotypes and expectations of others about where someone of her caliber should be. Instead, she followed her heart and her passion.

And she does it in a manner that is Better Than Perfect.

The quote on her personal notepad describes her approach beautifully: "If you want to go fast, go alone. If you want to go far, go together."

MAKE YOUR LIFE BIGGER THAN YOU

"I was complaining about how small my house was until I went down to a homeless shelter to volunteer," a client told me. "After that, I was sure grateful for having a place I could call my own."

People who have perfectionist tendencies—not to mention a good majority of nonperfectionists—can easily get so focused on their own personal worlds that they miss the big picture. We concentrate on what "needs" to be better in our lives, what we "should" do, what is not "up to standards," without taking a step back and asking, is this *really* how I want to direct my energy? Even, is this *really* what I believe?

BTP TIP: Increase Your Happiness
People who actively apply their spiritual beliefs to daily life enjoy stronger relationships and practice better health behaviors. They are more altruistic and helpful toward others, cope better with stress, and are happier.

"If you want to go fast, go alone. If you want to go far, go together."
—AFRICAN PROVERB

This stage in our journey together is a great time to talk about spirituality. While the terms "spirituality" and "religion" are often used interchangeably, *spirituality* does not mean *religion*. *Religion* can be defined as a specific, fundamental set of beliefs and practices generally agreed upon by a number of people. In contrast, "spirituality" is a more general term concerning less formal or structured belief systems and rituals. Spirituality is more about values and attitudes about life. Spirituality reminds us that there is more than meets the eye—that you are more than just your physical body. It includes a holistic appreciation of how everyone is connected in some way, each with his or her own contribution and purpose here on this earth.

Have you ever thought, "There has to be more to life that just this," or "I feel like something is missing from my life?" If so, you might find that exploring your spiritual views can be quite helpful.

Below is a series of important questions to ask yourself regarding your spirituality. Unlike a math quiz, there are no "right" or "wrong" answers here. What is important is that you start to explore your own beliefs, and how you can incorporate them into your life.

EXERCISE: MAKING YOUR LIFE BIGGER THAN YOU

What is your purpose here on earth? If that question is too overwhelming, what do you want your purpose to be?

_____

_____

_____

_____

_____

▶

Now consider what your life would be like if you believed the following state-ment: "Every experience has an ultimately positive purpose in my life." That word "ultimately" is vital because we all have had challenging, even trau-matic, experiences in our lives. And yet, good can come out of even horrific events. So, describe here what your life would be like if you believed that every experience had an ultimately positive purpose in your life.

_____

_____

_____

_____

_____

A CLIENT OF mine was in a terrible car accident that left him in a coma for weeks. Somehow he survived, after which he endured seven surgeries to rebuild the vital organs in his body. He went through more than a year of healing and rehabilitation. And yet, once it was over, he told me, "I am so grateful for that accident."

What?

He explained, "That accident was a wake-up call to remind me what is really important and what is not. Making more money so it could sit in some mutual fund was not what I really found valuable— even though that was how I had been living. I learned how much I love my family and friends, and how much they love me. My focus has completely changed. I am a new and much better man."

What do you believe? If you are a National Public Radio fan as I am, you may be familiar with their "This I Believe" campaign, which encourages listeners to share their deep-seated beliefs.

EXERCISE: "THIS I BELIEVE"

Write here three things that you believe.

1. _____

_____

_____

2. _____

_____

_____

3. _____

_____

_____

In his book *Your Next Big Thing: Ten Small Steps to Get Moving and Get Happy*, my friend Ben Michaelis, PhD, asks a powerful question. Okay, he actually poses lots of powerful questions. Here is one:

If you found you could make one lasting change in the world that would be guaranteed to affect people long after you were gone, what would that change be?

_____

_____

_____

Read over what you wrote in this section and reflect on it. Then write out your responses to the following questions.

In what you wrote, what are you most struck by? What stands out the most, is most surprising, or has the most meaning?

_____

_____

▶

_____

_____

_____

_____

What is one thing you can do today that will reflect your spiritual beliefs?

_____

_____

Have you identified one thing you can do today that reflects your spiritual beliefs? Well done; now go do it. And as you carry it out, focus on being present to *what* you are doing and *why* you are doing it. Allow yourself to be completely immersed in the activity—whether it be meditating, helping out others, spending time with a loved one, praying, taking a walk in nature—anything that reflects your spiritual beliefs.

Try not to judge how you look doing this, how well you are doing it, or how others may be perceiving you. Be mindful, in the now, so you can thoroughly enjoy this present you are giving to yourself.

When you apply your spiritual beliefs, you allow the authentic you to shine through. Distress—anger, shame, guilt, fear; judgment; and perfectionistic thinking all prevent the true you from being present.

TROUBLESHOOT THE ROADBLOCKS

Over the course of this book, you have identified new actions to cultivate your Better Than Perfect life. Of course, knowing where you want to go doesn't mean it will be easy to get there. If you plan to drive to

New York and have mapped out every mile of your trip, you may still come across unexpected construction, roadblocks, or detours. While these may require you to slightly alter your plans, don't let obstacles derail you completely.

> *Early in my career I worked in physical therapy. Being a physical therapist was one of the most rewarding and fulfilling jobs I could imagine. I helped clients get rid of severely disabling pain, taught people how to walk again after an accident or stroke, and helped people resume their favorite sport after an injury.*
>
> *My work with one client in particular changed my life. David was a fifty-six-year-old man whose diabetes had gotten out of control. As a result, a neuropathy developed in his leg that was so severe he had to have part of his leg amputated. After this David was assigned to the therapy gym to learn how to walk, use a prosthetic device, and generally function after his surgery.*
>
> *When I first met David, he was slumped over in his wheelchair. It was immediately evident that he wanted nothing to do with me or physical therapy. He grunted his responses to my questions. When I brought him over to the bars to get him walking for the first time since his surgery, he yelled at me, "Can't you just let me be?" Eventually I sent him back to his room.*
>
> *That afternoon I was doing rounds with the medical team. The doctor, nurses, physical therapist, occupational therapist, and nutritionist were all there, talking about the patients and*

how we could best help them as a team. When David's name came up, there was unanimous agreement that he was having difficulty coping and was feeling depressed.

The attending physician concluded David should be given Prozac.

The other members of the team nodded their heads in agreement. What? I was so stunned I couldn't move.

Here was a guy who had just lost his leg, and they were going to give him medication to deal with it. Wouldn't it make more sense to help him process what had happened? Help him talk through what he was experiencing? Help him find a new sense of who he was?

It was right then and there that I knew I had to go back to school to become a psychologist. I had to help people like David. Not everyone deals with the loss of a limb, but we all deal with some loss in our lives. I knew in my heart of hearts that was what I needed to do. What I didn't know was how challenging it would be.

Yes, a lot of obstacles presented themselves, such as going from making good money to owing over $40,000 a year. Also, clinical psychology is one of the toughest PhD programs to get into. (Luckily I didn't realize that at the time!) And, while most applicants already had a master's degree in psychology, I had taken only three psychology classes in my entire life.

There were also geographical and social obstacles. When I finally got into a program, it was a hundred miles away from my home, my friends, and my boyfriend.

*But those obstacles didn't prevent me from doing what I
knew I was meant to do.*

*I pursued this path from a place of strong passion and
desire: I wanted to help people dealing with loss, be it loss of
health, relationship, loved one, job, or way of life. I focused
on my passion rather than the obstacles. And, even though the
obstacles were there, I was able to transcend them.*

*Sure, I didn't do it the perfect way. I stumbled along the
way. Many times. And yet, driven by passion, I always knew
deep down that I was taking the right path for me. And, today, I'm so glad I did.*

How about you? What roadblocks might you encounter as you
transcend?

Let's look at some potential roadblocks, as well as how to overcome them.

The Goldilocks Syndrome: You're stressed about changing

Overwhelming stress can prevent us from being the people we want to
be. When our stress levels are high, we tend to think more negatively,
doubt our abilities, and revert back to old ways.

Of course, too little stress is not always a good thing either. Without
any stress, you might not be motivated to change. In this case, I'm not
talking about distress, but rather the state when things are not as you
desire. If life is going perfectly smoothly, then it's unlikely you will take
steps to improve. For a perfectionist, for example, it is important to be
in a place where you realize "This is not what I want," so that you'll
then be motivated to cultivate your Better Than Perfect life.

In the field of psychology, the Yerkes-Dodson Law contends that stress can improve performance up to a certain point. But, if you increase the stress past that point, performance decreases.

I call this the Goldilocks Syndrome: you don't want too much or too little. When it comes to stress levels, you want them "just right."

What to do: Use your stress to your advantage

Focus on *why* you want to make a change, particularly the changes you identified in Chapter 3: "The Price and Profits of Perfectionism." And take the steps necessary to reduce your stress both proactively and reactively. Make stress management a regular part of your day. This could involve getting a good night's sleep, eating a healthy diet, meditation, spending time with loved ones, and exercise.

Also, start a practice of regularly assessing your stress level on a scale of 0 to 10, where 0 is none and 10 is the highest it can be. Any time your stress is 7 or higher, take steps to effectively reduce your tension. Below are just a few of many possible means of stress reduction:

- Take some deep breaths.

- Move your body: jump on the bed (you have permission!), walk up a flight of stairs, dance around the room, do fifteen push-ups.

- Laugh: watch a funny video or read a joke.

- Listen to music.

- Hug a loved one.

- Play with your cat or dog.

What if . . . ? You're fearful and unsure about changing

Change can be scary for anyone, particularly a perfectionist who likes to *know* how things will work out. With change can come uncertainty. One client explained her fear like this:

> *"Even though I can see the benefits of making these changes and it makes sense that things could change, part of me is too scared to even try. What if it doesn't work? What if I invest all this time and energy, and things actually get worse? It's just easier to do what I've been doing for years. At least then I know what to expect."*

What to do: Get comfortable being uncomfortable

As we will discuss in this chapter's Action Steps below, it's important to face our fears. And one way to do that is to get more comfortable being uncomfortable. The best way to overcome your fears is to put yourself into situations where you may not feel 100 percent certain or calm. Try this out just a bit at a time. You'll likely find that it gets easier and easier.

Who am I kidding? You still criticize yourself in your head

Your inner critic may rear its ugly head, saying things like, "Who do you think you are?! You can't change. And if you do, it will mean the end of all the good you have. If you stop trying so hard, you will be even more of a failure." If you're anything like me you'll have heard negative self-talk like that in your mind too.

What to do: Say "Thanks but no thanks"

Realize that, while what you are saying to yourself may not feel good, the underlying motivation is positive. That voice is ultimately try-ing to protect you from being hurt. It wants you to feel good about yourself. Acknowledge that, appreciate the gesture, and then look for Better Than Perfect ways to feel good about yourself. (See "Exercise: Reframing Your Fearful Thoughts" in Chapter 10.)

And remember, the reason why what your inner critic says doesn't feel good is that it's not the genuine you speaking. So, choose thoughts that *do* feel right and good for you. Put on that custom-made jacket we talked about in Chapter 7: "Reinforce New Roads." Let your inner self-talk feel like a perfect fit for the real, amazing, wonderful you.

BTP TIP: Be Courageous

Keep in mind this quote from Meg Cabot in *The Princess Diaries*. (Okay, not a masterpiece, but still, this *is* a great quote!)

"Courage is not the absence of fear but the judgment that some-thing else is more important than fear. The brave may not live forever but the cautious do not live at all. For now you are traveling the road between who you think you are and who you can be."

Life is nothing like the brochure: Your circumstances seem too difficult

Author Jodi Picoult once wrote, "That's what happens to dreams, life gets in the way."

I say, "Only if you let it."

Yes, circumstances may arise that challenge you in transcending. Many of these events may be outside of your control. That does not mean you need to throw away your dreams and go back to the life you had before.

What to do: Persevere

- Review that list of *why* you want to change and what your new life will be like when you do (your "Why You Want to Kick But" exercise in Chapter 9: "Eliminate Extremes"). Keep in mind the emotional, physical, social, work, financial, and spiritual benefits you will gain and cherish.

- Reach out to a close friend or confidant for assistance.

- Soar above life's obstacles by using the visualization at the end of this chapter.

They won't let me change: You're worried people will be upset with you

As you take this Better Than Perfect voyage, family, friends, coworkers, even strangers may not react the way you want them to. But if people in your life get upset, complain about your new ways, make hurtful comments, or do things that disturb or undermine you, it does not mean you need to stop and revert back to old, troubling behaviors or habits.

What to do: Take control

Acknowledge that the modifications you are making may be affecting those around you, too. Realize that change can be hard for others, even if that change is ultimately positive. Help the people around you to better understand why you are doing what you are doing.

When Emily came to see me, she worked fourteen-hour days. Her team could always count on getting a response from her within minutes, even on weekends. She was the one who would take on tough projects, devote countless hours, and instinctively take up slack from other team members.

"My team knew I would pretty much do anything at any time."

As the result of our working together, Emily started implementing some balance in her life. She set limits regarding what times she would work, when she would check her emails, and what projects she would do. Although she still did much more than her job description required, she was not working as much as she did before.

Not surprisingly, these changes upset her coworkers. Emily described some of the reactions she received. "Jim asked me in an extremely sarcastic tone, 'And will we be able to get ahold of Princess Emily this weekend or will she be too busy?'"

When Emily declined a meeting scheduled for 6:00 PM about, as she put it, "a topic we could easily discuss the next day during business hours," another colleague reminded her that their boss would be on the call. "It was like she was threatening to tattle on me."

Rather than put up with the various aggressive and passive-aggressive reactions her life changes had garnered, Emily chose to meet with a few key people individually to explain what she was doing and why.

"I used your example," she told me, "of professional athletes who train hard and rest hard in order to perform their best. I told one boss I wanted to be even better at work—and in my personal life. We talked about how inefficient we both get when we're tired or really stressed. I asked him to let me give this a try to see how it worked. He agreed."

Soon, Emily was able to prove to her colleagues that she really could do more with less.

You really can do more with less.

If people in your life object to your changes, try calmly but assertively to share your new approach and how it will ultimately benefit both you and them. Most likely, they'll appreciate that their feelings have been acknowledged and will understand what you're doing. Maybe they'll even take your example to improve their own lives.

SET EMOTIONAL LIMITS

Just because you *can* work for another two hours doesn't mean it makes sense to do so.

Just because you *can* work out every day doesn't mean it's healthy.

Just because you *can* do other people's work rather than delegate doesn't mean that's what is best.

Just because you *can* take the toughest road doesn't mean it's necessarily the *best* road.

Just because you can doesn't mean you should.

I remember a conversation I had with a few friends many years ago. One friend was pregnant and talking about having a natural childbirth. "I mean, I'm sure I can handle it," she told us.

My other friend responded, "Why? You're not going to get a medal for it. Your child will never stop and thank you for the pain you went through by not getting an epidural."

I bring up this conversation not as a means to deliberate on the pros and cons of natural childbirth, but rather because it made me (who had not yet had any children) think. I wondered if there were things I did just to prove to myself and others that I could do them, even if I didn't actually want to do them.

How about you? Can you think of anything you do in your life that's more motivated by a desire to prove your capability than by a desire to enjoy yourself? Is there anything you do just to prove to others that you can?

One example I found concerned my clinical practice. I would schedule as many clients as possible at whatever times they wanted so as to work with the most clients possible. Part of that approach had to do with revenue. Another part had to do with wanting to help as many people as possible. Still another part of me did this because I could. And so, in my mind, I should.

What I found, though, was that this scheduling was a challenge, in terms of both time and energy.

So, I started to set limits on the times I would see clients. By establishing office hours, I no longer saw clients in the evenings or on weekends. Sure, I could have made more money and helped more individuals with more hours, but at what price?

And, in reality, while I may have lost a few clients because of this, I found that most respected the hours and simply accepted them.

Next, I realized that I needed to set limits on my energy, too. Some clients require more psychological energy than others. This is not to say they are "bad" clients; they are just more energetically needy. Rather than expect myself to be "perfect," able to provide exactly what my clients needed whenever it was convenient for them, I started to schedule certain clients on different days so as to stagger throughout the week the appointments that needed "more" from me.

I came to realize that I don't have to prove anything to anyone. Taking care of my own energy—emotional, mental, physical, and even spiritual—is more important to me than "doing it all."

This same idea applies to other occupations as well. Consider doctors, nurses, nursing assistants, social workers, accountants, coaches, personal trainers, physical therapists, occupational therapists, attorneys, stay-at-home moms. They all need to take care of their needs so they can best take care of ours.

How about you? What limits do you want to establish in your life? Perhaps the times you'll work and the times when you'll play? Or how people may speak to you? Or what projects you take on?

This is not to say that you will slack on doing your job or fulfilling your responsibilities. This is to say there's a way to achieve what you want in a manner that works best—both for you and, ultimately, for those around you too.

YOU ARE NOT STUCK!

Do you ever feel as if people around you hold you back, like quicksand sucking you in? Living a Better Than Perfect life entails not only being able to change how you view and interact with the world, but also being able to influence how others relate to you. Your words and actions serve as a model for how others view and interact with you.

By being intentional in what you say and do, you can impact others' thoughts and behaviors.

In Emily's example above, we saw how communicating with others is important for helping them understand and even support you. You can take it a step further by holding others accountable for the boundaries you set.

A self-made millionaire by his early twenties, Darren Hardy is a New York Times *best-selling author, publisher, and editorial director of* Success *magazine, as well as one of my personal mentors. His business advice goes beyond focusing on finances. He truly gets the psychological concepts central to a thriving business.*

"You teach people how to treat you," he once told me.

You know those people who are always late? And not just a few minutes, but twenty, thirty minutes or longer? Well, guess what? You can control that. Sure, you can get upset with them, but that usually doesn't do much good in the long run.

Here's how Darren handled a similar situation. "I was supposed to meet my buddy for dinner. He's notoriously late for every meeting or event. After ten minutes he hadn't shown up, so I got in my car and left. While I was driving home he called my cell. 'I'm here,' he said. 'Where are you?'

"'On my way home,' I told him. 'I waited and you didn't show, so I left.'

"By now, it was about thirty minutes after we were supposed to have met up. 'Well I'm here now,' he said. 'Come on back.'"

Darren's reply? "Nope." And he continued his journey home.

Guess how late his friend was the next time they were scheduled to meet? Not at all.

"He's still late for everyone else," Darren chuckled, "but not with me."

BTP TIP: Aggressive Versus Assertive

Clients often tell me they don't want to upset anyone, so they keep quiet when they're unhappy about something. The trouble is, we can only hold in our feelings for so long before they spill out—and those spills can cause harm. So it's important to differentiate between the aggressive and the assertive approaches to interacting with others. It is possible to stand up for yourself without being aggressive.

* *Assertive* means directly communicating your own wants and needs while still being respectful toward others.

* *Aggressive* refers to communicating your wants and needs in a manner that's disrespectful to others.

* *Passive* means suppressing your own wants and needs so as to avoid being unkind to others.

* *Passive-aggressive* refers to indirectly communicating what you want or need in a way that is disrespectful to others.

It's important to be assertive—to stand up for your own rights while still being respectful to others. Darren was not *aggressive*—he didn't argue with his friend or yell at him. He was not *passive*, refusing to say anything while holding in his frustration. He was not *passive-aggressive,* saying something like, "Thanks for *finally* deciding to show up." None of these three approaches would have been helpful to Darren or his friend.

Which approach to interacting with others do you think would best suit your Better Than Perfect life? Being assertive allows you to express what you want without being disrespectful. Consider how you may have handled the type of situation Darren described.

EXERCISE: REFLECTING ON HOW WE INTERACT WITH OTHERS

Think back on experiences when you felt hostage to other people's reactions.

Can you recall an incident when you were aggressive? Describe it here.

_____

_____

_____

Can you recall an incident when you were passive?

_____

_____

_____

Can you recall an incident when you were passive-aggressive?

_____

_____

_____

Now, for one of the incidents you've described, write out how you could have been more assertive instead.

_____

_____

_____

Don't beat yourself up with this information; rather use it when future opportunities arise.

In addition to being true to yourself, hold others accountable for boundaries you establish.

ACTION STEPS

Step 1: *Get Comfortable Being Uncomfortable*

Step 2: *Change Your "But" to "And"*

Step 3: *Do Social Good*

Final Step: *Soar!*

Step 1: Get Comfortable Being Uncomfortable

Years ago I taught a Spin class. I used to tell my students to "get comfortable being uncomfortable." Why? For three reasons. One, what initially feels uncomfortable, when done repeatedly, eventually fails to cause discomfort. In essence, it becomes the new normal. Two, the more accustomed you get to trying new things, the more you actually try new things. And three, the more you venture out into the unknown, the more you can make positive changes in your life.

"Intrigue expert" and world-renowned author and keynote speaker Sam Horn developed the following three-stage framework for change:

1. Awkward

2. Apply

3. Automatic

Hold others accountable for boundaries you establish.

First Stage of Change: Awkward

At first, what is new feels *awkward*—just like when you got behind the wheel of a car for the first time. I bet it felt strange, and you likely felt unsure about how much pressure to put on the brake, turn the steering wheel, or even twist the key. In this first stage of change, you might feel embarrassed or uncomfortable. Here's what this stage was like for a client of mine:

> *Jennifer had the mind-set "I need to keep my phone on so I can check my emails during the night, just in case a client reaches out." This regular pattern disrupted her sleep and left her feeling tired the following day.*
>
> *As one step in her Better Than Perfect journey, Jennifer decided to allow herself to shut off her phone at ten at night and not turn it back on again until six the next morning.*
>
> *When we spoke after her first night she told me, "It was really hard for me. I kept wanting to check my email. What if someone needed some information from me? Would they think I was slacking off?"*

Often, people who experience Jennifer's difficulty stop at that point and revert back to old ways. "It was too stressful," they might say, or, "It does not *feel* genuine." And, while that's likely true, it doesn't mean this new way is not right for you. When a change feels awkward to you, try to reframe how you interpret that awkwardness. Remind yourself: "Hey, this is the first part of making lasting change. It's supposed to feel awkward. That means I'm right on track."

Second Stage of Change: Apply

In the next stage of change you *apply* your chosen skill or new behavior. At this stage the change seems less awkward, but it's still a conscious behavior that calls for intentional focus. In our driving example, this stage is when turning the steering wheel and pressing on the brake feel easier but still require you to pay attention.

It is during these early stages that we're especially prone to giving up all together. Consider Rich's story.

Rich had a hard time delegating. Despite being a manager, he had a strong tendency to do a lot of the tactical work usually performed by employees. When he started the process of relaxing some of his micromanaging, he noticed that one of his team members, now doing a task Rich had previously done, did what he considered to be subpar work.

"His crappy work is a poor reflection on me. Now I have to do it all over again and I only have a day to get it done. It would've been much easier for me to just do this all myself from the beginning."

After empathizing with Rich's stress, I asked him, "What could you do to improve the project and still not do it all yourself?"

Rich looked at me with annoyance. "Well, I could teach him how to do it right, but that would take even more time. Time is something I do not have."

"And if you taught him how to do it this time, how would that affect things in the future?" I continued.

"Well, he would be able to do it himself next time," Rich offered. "In fact, this is something he could do for most of the projects we work on. Plus, I guess he would be more likely to own that part of the project. Now that I think of it, my team is so used to me doing everything that they probably sometimes only do a half-assed job because they know I'll fix it."

By thinking this through, Rich realized the value in persevering with his change—holding his team more responsible for their work—rather than simply reverting back to his old ways. While persevering meant he had some more training to do, which would take more time in the short term, the plan ultimately freed up a lot of time and energy in the long run.

Can you relate?

EXERCISE: APPLYING CHANGE IN YOUR LIFE

When did you apply the Better Than Perfect strategies—implementing a change in your life—only to get an outcome you did not completely want?

_____

_____

_____

_____

_____

_____

_____

_____

What did you do to stay on track? Or what could you do next time?

_____

_____

_____

_____

_____

_____

_____

_____

Once you get comfortable being uncomfortable, it won't be so uncomfortable.

Third Stage of Change: Automatic

When you stick with a new behavior long enough, it eventually becomes *automatic*. This is the final stage of change. You no longer need to think about doing it; you simply do it—just as you drive your own car. And when something happens that you don't want, you focus on how to make it better. At this stage, the option of giving up doesn't appear.

For example, if you were driving a specific car model for the first time, you might notice as you were decelerating that you needed to push more gently on the brake than you're used to. That realization doesn't keep you from slowing down, nor does it incline you to give up on trying out new car models. It simply cues you to make a slight adjustment in the new car—and to keep driving.

Step 2: Change Your "But" to "And"

Don't let a big "but" get in your way.

Remember those "buts" you kicked in Chapter 9? Well, we're not done yet. Do the following sound familiar?

- "I want to change, but . . ."

- "I thought about doing that, but . . ."

- "I tried, but . . ."

- "I would do that, but . . ."

- "That sounds good, but . . ."

When we hear the word "but," we tend to treat it like a thousand-ton obstacle that cannot be removed. *But* means, "This is set in stone and there is nothing you can do." As a result, we believe and accept that we can't change whatever the "but" dictates and feel powerless against it.

Here's a newsflash: you don't have to be controlled by a "but." In fact, you can actually use your big "but" to achieve the goal you want.

How? Replace the word "but" with "and."

"I feel like I'm going crazy at home."

Those were Missy's first words when we started working together.

She described her love for her family, as well as a lot of stress at home with her two young children. As we explored what was going on, it became evident that Missy's perfectionism was causing her to be short with the kids and her husband.

"I get so frustrated when my kids act up," she told me. "I want to keep my cool, but I also want them to know how important the rules are."

This was a great opportunity for Missy to change her "buts" into "ands."

Missy's statement, "I want to keep my cool, but I also want them to know how important the rules are," was transformed to "I want to keep my cool and I want them to know how important the rules are." This conscious determination prompted Missy to take steps to address her stress before she spoke to her children about their behavior.

She chose to see her parenting as a puzzle. She needed to try fitting various pieces together before finding the right match. Instead of all-or-nothing thinking ("If they act up,

*they will never follow the rules"), she decided to see parenting
as a work in progress, with each incident giving her new information as to which piece goes where.*

The result? Less stress and better parenting.

How can you apply this concept in your life?

_____

Don't let a big "but" get in your way.

_____

EXERCISE: TRANSFORMING "BUT" INTO "AND"

Write out what "buts" you have in your life right now. Then replace them
with "and." Use the new statement to identify steps you can take to make
what you want happen.

OLD "BUT"	NEW "AND"	NOW I WILL...
I want to change but	I want to change and	
I thought about doing that but	I thought about doing that and	

▶

OLD "BUT"	NEW "AND"	NOW I WILL...
I tried but	I tried and	
Add your own here:		

Step 3: Do Social Good

Helping out others does wonders for them—and for ourselves. In fact, doing social good can improve our happiness, health, relationships, fun, spiritual health, and even work.

I often hear clients say, "I want to volunteer but . . ."

This is a great opportunity for replacing a "but" with an "and." It's also an important reminder that anything you do for the common good is better than doing nothing. Doing social good doesn't have to mean donating a million dollars or working in Africa for three weeks, or even volunteering every week. It doesn't have to be perfect; you can make it Better Than Perfect.

Don't have a lot of money? Giving a dollar to a good cause is still a contribution, and is added to the single dollars of others just like you.

(Along the same lines: though get you only one vote, it's still worth it to vote, since our collective votes add up.) Don't have a lot of time? Let's say a nonprofit doing work you believe in is sponsoring an event. Tweeting, Facebooking, or sharing the info with your social network could be helpful to your cause, and wouldn't take that much time.

EXERCISE: VOLUNTEERING YOUR VALUES

Don't know what cause you want to further? Use some of what you came up with in the "Making Your Life Bigger Than You" exercise earlier in this chapter to help you figure out what resonates for you. Then answer the questions below.

What are some possible paths you could explore?

_____

_____

_____

Don't know which group you want to help out? Find out what's available in your area. Organizations like VolunteerMatch (www.volunteermatch.org) are great resources for helping you find the right match for your skills and interests.

Don't have enough time to fully commit yet? HandsOn Network (www .handsonnetwork.org) offers many "done in a day" volunteer opportunities. Try working on a few different projects to see what strikes your fancy and where you feel most at home.

Find out what volunteer opportunities are available in your area. Then, note here three projects or groups that interest you:

1. _____

2. _____

3. _____

▶

Now, imagine yourself involved, even for just part of a day, in one or more of the groups or projects you listed. Record here at least one opportunity you're willing to pursue further.

_____

_____

_____

Next, identify the first step in getting started (submitting an email expressing your interest, attending an information session, signing up for training, etc.).

_____

_____

_____

For example, one of my passions is helping people learn the skills to have a happier, more resilient life with greater meaning. One of the ways I apply that is by conducting workshops and trainings for groups who have faced serious challenges. Working with groups such as Gilda's Club (for people with cancer), Dress for Success, and the ALS Association (helping folks with Lou Gehrig's Disease) has brought so much meaning into my life, and I hope it has helped others.

Final Step: Soar!

It is your time to soar, to transcend the old way of thinking and acting, to release your inner critic and the negative self-talk, doubt, guilt, shame, anger, frustration, helplessness, and worthlessness. It's your time to be who you were created to be: Better Than Perfect.

The following is a visualization to help you soar. Read it and then close your eyes and visualize. Or, ask a friend to read it to you, or record yourself reading it so you can visualize it as you listen to the recording. You can also download a free recording at www.ElizabethLombardo .com/BetterThanPerfect.

EXERCISE: VISUALIZING YOURSELF SOARING

Find a cozy spot to sit where there are no distractions. Get into a comfortable position and close your eyes. Take a few slow, deep breaths. Focus on the breath coming in on your inhale and out during the exhale.

Give yourself permission to take a few moments out of your day to focus on you.

Now start to relax your body and mind. As you focus on your inhale and exhale, relax your body. Notice that the top of your head, your forehead, your mouth, and your jaw are starting to relax even more.

Notice your neck relaxing more, your shoulder muscles relaxing. Your shoulders may even drop a little bit.

Feel the relaxation going from your shoulders, down to your elbows, to your hands, to each of your fingers.

Notice the relaxation going down your chest and your stomach, down your neck and your back, so that your entire torso starts to relax more now.

Your legs are starting to relax: your hips, your calves, your feet, and each of your toes. Enjoy your entire body relaxing even more now with each soothing breath you take.

As you're enjoying the relaxation in your mind and body, imagine yourself sitting outside. You may be at a beach, in a meadow, or in a park. You can be wherever you want to be.

As you are sitting in a supportive chair, you recline back, allowing your body to relax even more. Now, look up at the sky. The sky is a beautiful vibrant blue, dotted with soft puffy clouds. Watch as the clouds slowly move across the blue sky.　▶

As you relax into your chair, close your eyes and smile.

Think about all the wonderful changes you have made in your life.

You are living a Better Than Perfect life.

What does it look like?

How does it feel to love yourself unconditionally? To love others unconditionally?

What does your body feel like?

How do others react to the loving and grateful new you?

What does it feel like to know that you are enough—that you don't have to do or be any more than you are?

You are so grateful. Your relationships are strong. You feel true contentment, satisfaction, and happiness.

How you spend your time has become more fun. You are full of passion.

At the same time, you've become much more productive.

Reflect upon the positive changes in your work, your relationships, and your health.

You feel so much more connected to who you are and to your purpose here on earth.

You never knew you could feel this good.

You never realized you could be at such peace.

Your entire mind and body are relaxed, optimistic, and full of pure joy.

You are proud of the life that you've created. You are proud of the person you have become.

You marvel at how the people in your life have changed: your loved ones, your friends, even your coworkers are happier.

You are so grateful for the incredible changes you have made.

Smile as you experience this gratitude and appreciation for your life that is Better Than Perfect.

Now commit to this vision. Commit to choosing passion over fear. Commit to creating the life you love. Commit to living a Better Than Perfect life.

Epilogue

BETTER THAN PERFECT

Wow, here we are at the end of the book. But we are not at the end of our journey. Just as a golfer cannot read a book about the sport and expect to automatically drop his handicap, we also need to practice and continue coaching ourselves to truly create the lives we want.

This is a new way of living for many of us. As such, we need to develop new habits, and continue to practice them.

When I was in high school, I was not a big fan of working out. Sure, I knew it was good for me, but it was not high on my "What I want to do" list.

In college, I started going to a gym. At first I forced myself to go. But within a year I looked forward to my workouts. I even started teaching classes. Fast-forward, and for over half of my life exercising has been a part of my (almost) daily routine.

My reaction to exercise went from "Ugh" to "I feel like I need to do it but it feels weird" to "This is an important and enjoyable part of my life."

Releasing perfectionistic patterns and living a Better Than Perfect life was similar for me. In addition to wanting to be happier, I was motivated by wanting to practice what I preach. How could I authentically help others when I was not willing to do similar work and improve my life, too?

A few years ago, as I was considering writing a book about perfectionism, I was chatting with Stacy London, the co-host of the long-running show What Not to Wear. *She had just written a book called* The Truth About Style, *in which she talked about fashion as well as about the stories behind people's lives.*

Also included was some of her own story, which included her struggle with being underweight and then, by some standards, overweight.

I asked her, "What's it like to just let it all hang out? To tell people some of the not-so-perfect parts of your life?"

With a thoughtful smile she responded, "It actually feels good." She then explained how stressful it can be to pretend that you are perfect, to try to appear as if you are put together all the time.

I realized that I wanted to do the same. I wanted to celebrate being human rather than pretending to be perfect.

Can you relate?

You are not alone. There is a strong desire in our society to be Better Than Perfect, to stop trying to be something we are not.

Actress Jennifer Lawrence is a great example. From her no-nonsense say-what-you-think interviews to her stumble and fall at both the 2013 and 2014 Oscars, Jennifer oozes Better Than Perfect, and that's one of the ingredients that makes her so attractive.

SO, HOW'S IT GOING?

So, how are things going with you in your Better Than Perfect journey? If you're like many people, you've been able to apply some of the concepts some of the time.

You also might be thinking:

- "Why can't I do this?"

- "If it's not broken, why fix it?"

- "I understand the rationale, but I have trouble actually implementing the strategies."

- "I'm scared that it will have negative consequences."

- "I tried one of the strategies, but it didn't really work."

- "I'll give it a try when things calm down in my life."

Any of these sound familiar to you?

Let's look at each one separately.

"Why can't I do this?"

You *can* live a Better Than Perfect life. Be patient with yourself. This may be an entirely new way of thinking and acting for you. Remember, if your ultimate goal is to get to the top of the Empire State Building, with each step up you are moving in the right direction.

Be proud of yourself for taking the time to learn this new approach.

Pick *one* strategy to start implementing today. The "Where Do You Go From Here?" section later in this chapter can help you choose which one. Be your own cheerleader, not a drill sergeant.

"If it's not broken, why fix it?"

Remember life before cell phones? Or, if you are too young for that, remember life before the iPad or similar tablets? It's not as if you were miserable before having 24/7 access to the world thanks to a computer that fit in your bag. And yet, now that this technology is in your life, you probably can't imagine living without it again.

Some of you reading this book might think, "I'm doing just fine the way things are. No need to make a change."

In reality, when you apply the concepts in this book, your life will transform into something you can barely imagine, something truly amazing. Imagine a life of joy, passion, and unconditional love for yourself! Start applying the concepts presented here today to reap the much deserved benefits.

"I understand the rationale, but I have trouble actually implementing the strategies."

Many of my clients tell me, "I know what I want to do when we're talking about it, but then life happens. I just don't seem to do it."

Stress is often the culprit. When you're in a situation or environment where your stress is lower, it's easier to rationally consider which Better Than Perfect strategies you want to use. When stress levels are high, though, we tend to think in old, more self-defeating patterns. That's when your subconscious is most likely to be shouting at you: "Yeah, you thought that new thing would work, but let's stick with our old ways."

Here's one way to combat this. Whenever you experience perfectionist thinking, behaviors, or even associated feelings, stop and ask yourself: "On a scale from 0 to 10, what is my stress level right now?"

At a stress level of 7 or above, rational thinking can go out the door, which leaves you less able to pursue the life you want. So, anytime your stress measures 7 or higher, stop what you're doing and take steps to reduce your stress in a healthy and helpful way. Perhaps you could:

- Take some deep breaths.

- Laugh.

- Listen to a fun song that makes you want to get up and dance around.

- Move your body: do jumping jacks, jog in place, go for a quick walk.

One of my clients immediately drops to the floor and pumps out twenty-five push-ups whenever she realizes her stress has gotten too high. How you reduce your stress level is up to you. When you get it back down again, you'll be better able to think and act in new, more helpful ways.

"I'm scared that it will have negative consequences."

A common remark I hear from my clients is "I understand what you are saying, but . . ." While they may acknowledge that perfectionism has had some negative consequences, at the same time they also believe that perfectionism has been the force behind their many successes.

Remember, we're not talking about getting rid of what truly works for you. The goal is to keep the dedication, perseverance, resilience, and tenacity that make you strive for excellence. At the same time, you want to be loving toward yourself and stop the barrage of negative self-talk. While mentally beating yourself up may help motivate you in some ways, it also prevents you from functioning optimally in the world.

Better Than Perfect strategies provide a new way to speak to yourself, a new way to view yourself, a new way to interact with people you love and the other people around you, and a new way to live in which you keep the motivation and drop the self-destruction.

When in doubt, go back to Chapter 3: "The Price and Profits of Perfectionism" and review your PCPC assessment.

"I tried one of the strategies, but it didn't really work."

Great! First, congratulate yourself on the time, energy, and effort you gave to try out a new strategy. Then use what happened as data.

Remember, when something doesn't go the way you planned, it's not a failure; rather it's data you can use to help you get the results you want. So, what prevented the outcome you desired? Lack of practice? High stress? Too little time? Fear?

Once you identify the ingredients preventing the outcome you want, take steps to adjust your recipe for the future.

"I'll give it a try when things calm down in my life."
And when will that be? About half past never? Life can be hectic, busy, action-packed, even a little crazy . . . Waiting until things calm down may mean waiting until your heart stops beating.

Rather than waiting until your world is less crazy, remember that these Better Than Perfect strategies will help you reduce the turmoil in your life. They will help you do more in less time and with less energy. They will help you enjoy life more and stress less. They will help you live a life of passion and excitement rather than anxiety and defeat. The sooner you start, the sooner you will enjoy the benefits, and the easier it will become.

WHERE DO YOU GO FROM HERE?

If you're not yet exactly where you want to be, don't give up. You can go back through all seven strategies in the order they were presented here. Or, pick a chapter that really spoke to you and start there. You can also look at the specific actions presented throughout the book and pursue the ones that would be most impactful for you.

To take this latter approach, it may be helpful to assess where you are in the Better Than Perfect lifestyle.

EXERCISE: WHERE ARE YOU IN THE BETTER THAN PERFECT SPECTRUM?

On a scale from 0 to 10, where 0 is "Never" and 10 is "More than once a day," rate how often you do the following:

P: POSTMORTEM YOUR PAST	
Feel the "need" to use your perfectionistic patterns.	

E: EVALUATE YOUR EXPECTATIONS	
Feel entitled.	
Get upset when someone else does not follow your rules.	
Catch yourself saying or thinking *should*.	
Experience guilt or shame.	
Feel angry or resentful toward others.	

R: REINFORCE NEW ROADS	
Catch yourself in self-defeating thinking.	
Have a high level of stress.	
Try affirmations that don't work.	
"Put your winter coat on in summer."	
Wear the proverbial "stinky coat": owning your own or other people's negativity.	
Catch yourself using distorted thinking.	
Regret the past.	
Worry about the future.	

▶

F: FAIL FORWARD	
Fear failing.	
Find yourself motivated by fear instead of passion.	
Avoid or procrastinate doing things.	
Engage in an activity with what others may view as excessive time or energy.	

E: ELIMINATE EXTREMES	
Use "extreme" words, such as *never* and *always*.	
Mind-read: assume you know what others are thinking.	
Base your worth on others' reactions.	
Base your worth on your accomplishments.	
Minimize your achievements.	
Feel like giving up.	
Try to deal with life on your own without reaching out for support.	

C: CREATE, DON'T COMPARE	
Compare yourself to others.	
Feel in competition with others.	
Base your worth on how hard you worked.	
Avoid hobbies/areas of interest because you don't "have time" or see them as frivolous.	
Avoid relaxing or playing with friends.	
Focus on what you don't want instead of feeling grateful for what you already have.	

▶

T: TRANSCEND	
Feel as if there is something missing in your life or there must be something more.	
Have trouble implementing the Better Than Perfect strategies.	
Feel like a hostage to other people because of their actions or energy.	
Use the word "but."	
Have trouble envisioning a Better Than Perfect life.	

Now, go back through this chart and circle or highlight any rating of 4 or higher.

You've just created your Better Than Perfect to-do list! For each highlighted item, go back and review the corresponding chapter, or at least the section in the chapter that discusses that topic.

A BETTER THAN PERFECT EXAMPLE

As I was trying to think of a story to share during this send-off, my high school reunion came to mind. Perfectionism can keep you from fully enjoying milestone events like reunions—even from attending them. And, since the first strategy chapter included how my pattern of perfectionism started in school, it seems only fitting that we end by discussing a reunion with the same fellow students.

> *"That must be a typo," I thought as I looked at the invitation for my high school reunion. "There is no way it's been twenty-five years."*
>
> *Guess I was wrong.*

For all of those who are trying to do the math (I know I would be), I graduated high school in 1988, which makes me forty-three as of this writing.

Do I want to go back for the reunion? I wondered. In the past, my perfectionism might have kept me from attending, or at least might have caused serious stress if I did decide to go. But instead, I felt true excitement about seeing old friends.

Thinking about going back to see my classmates, I decided to **postmortem my past.** *In reflecting upon previous reunions, I realized just how many of my fears had never been realized. Rather than being judgmental or superficial, ready to criticize me the moment I walked in, these women from my all-girls high school were excited to reunite and learn about what others had been up to over the years. Previous cliques had dissolved. The focus was more on laughing as a group about past events than on poking fun at anyone.*

Before going, I **evaluated my expectations.** *Instead of predetermining how the other women would react, I chose to focus on having fun. I concentrated on ways to experience and share gratitude and love with these incredible women, now successful attorneys, teachers, businesswomen, editors, heads of nonprofits—and most of us moms to boot.*

I chose to **reinforce new roads** *by being present and enjoying the moment instead of critiquing myself over what I said, did, or looked like.*

*I also decided to **fail forward,** releasing fears that I would say something ridiculous or mess up in some way, determining in advance I wouldn't stress about making a mistake.*

*In order to **eliminate extremes,** I decided not to label myself or others, especially not negatively.*

*I chose to **create** an experience of fun **rather than compare** myself to the other women. Where they were in their lives versus where I am in mine is of no consequence; all that mattered was whether we felt happy and content where we were. When I ran into a woman who'd given me a hard time twenty-five years ago, I realized that her actions back then were a reflection of how she had felt—and had nothing to do with me.*

*Overall I also **transcended** my fears, felt empowered by how I chose to react, and reveled in reconnecting with some truly incredible people. Rather than being paralyzed with perfectionism, I soared with true joy. I have wonderful memories of that reunion, as well as rekindled friendships that I cherish.*

Landmark events like reunions can provide a sort of Rorschach test of how you feel about yourself and your life. Can you imagine experiencing a landmark event as the quintessential and satisfied you? You could enjoy yourself without letting perfectionism get in the way.

With conscious practice applying the Better Than Perfect strategies, many of my clients have achieved this; to say that the difference they've experienced is dramatic would be an understatement.

WHILE THIS MAY be the end of this chapter, please don't let it be the end of your pursuit and application of a Better Than Perfect life. Keep this book where you will frequently see it: next to your bed, in the kitchen, on your desk. During the day, open it up to a page and take five minutes to reread a portion; doing this will help you keep these principles in mind. Apply the Action Steps. You can also print out the Better Than Perfect quotes at www.ElizabethLombardo.com /BetterThanPerfect. Some find it helpful to post different quotes in different spots where they'll see them regularly.

Let's take it a step further. Let's start a conversation—even a movement—to encourage our loved ones, and that includes ourselves, to be Better Than Perfect. What if, rather than pointing out faults, we embraced the ways that we live a Better Than Perfect life?

What are those ways? Some of the answers to that question appeared in a speech at the Black Women in Hollywood Luncheon hosted by *Essence* magazine. Oscar winner Lupita Nyong'o spoke of beauty: "What is fundamentally beautiful is compassion for yourself and for those around you. That kind of beauty enflames the heart and enchants the soul."

Compassion is Better Than Perfect.

Love is Better Than Perfect.

Passion is Better Than Perfect.

A life of purpose is Better Than Perfect.

Happiness is Better Than Perfect.

EXERCISE: WHAT IS BETTER THAN PERFECT FOR YOU?

What areas in your life are Better Than Perfect? Complete the following sentence:

_____

. . . is Better Than Perfect.

I'd like to share with you some of the answers clients and friends have shared with me:

- Chicken nuggets for dinner are Better Than Perfect.

- A ten-minute walk for exercise is Better Than Perfect.

- My relatively tidy home is Better Than Perfect.

- Hair up in a ponytail is Better Than Perfect.

Share your Better Than Perfect statements with friends, social media, and the world.

You were born Better Than Perfect. And then you got in your own way; your inner critic took over. This is the time to crush your inner critic and create the life you love. As a result, you will be more accepting and satisfied, more successful, more joyful and balanced.

Choose to release the chains of perfectionism . . .

Choose to love yourself, your life, and those around you unconditionally.

Choose to be the amazing individual you were created to be.

Choose to live a Better Than Perfect life.

Acknowledgments

THIS BOOK WOULD be nothing more than a thought in my head if it were not for a host of amazing individuals.

Thank you to my agent J. L. Stermer, Laura Mazer, and the folks at Seal Press for helping me find the right home for *Better Than Perfect*. To Stephanie Abarbanel and Kirsten Janene-Nelson, thanks for your Charlie Brown Christmas tree edits that helped make this book shine. And, Andrew Frothingham, thanks for jumping in, too.

I am so grateful to those who contributed stories to this book, including Jordan Kemper, Marilyn King, Vince Poscente, Donna Towle, Stacy London, the folks at Weight Watchers and Ketchum, and the countless others whose identity was kept confidential. To my clients who teach me so much, please know that you are all more similar than you can imagine. The cases shared were often a conglomerate of what so many of you are dealing with. Thank you for trusting me and including me on your incredible journey.

So many people have offered advice, support, and love. These include Rachel DeAlto, Marci Shimoff, Debra Poneman, Wendy Lipton Dibner, Darren Weissman, Mary O'Donohue, Jeremy and

Natlia Remmy, Camper Bull, Jennifer Blake, Kimberly Rose, Patti and John Haslett, Michael Lombardo, Karen Swanson, Carrie and Dave Gaston, Nina Brown, Diana and Chris Webb, Natasha Backes, Scott and Amy Gray, Chris Lane, Sue and Kevin Boroch, and the beloved Julie Woods.

THANK YOU TO the amazing mentors I have had in my life: Drs. Arthur and Christine Maguth Nezu, Steve Harrison, Brendon Burchard, and Darren Hardy. And to the amazing Sam Horn, my writing and marketing coach—so much of this book has your magical touch on it.

Thank you to my incredible team—Shelton Mercer III, Kelly Taylor, Envy McKee, Melody Harstine-Foster, Jim Olen, Candi Carter, and Bill Cashman. Your devotion and passion will allow us to make this world a better place—now and for future generations. And to all of the wonderful reporters and producers who have helped me spread my messages to millions, I am so grateful.

To my mom, dad, and sister, Martha, thank you for your never-ending love and support. I really lucked out when it comes to love from my gene pool. To my friends and colleagues throughout my life, thanks for putting up with my perfectionism and still loving me.

Kelly and Gracie, I am so honored to be your mother and so grateful for the love we all share. It is because of you that I want to be Better Than Perfect.

And last but not least, to Jeffrey, who somehow saw the true me underneath the mud of perfectionism. Your love, sense of humor, and passion for life are a true gift. Thank you!

Notes

CHAPTER ONE

For example, research: Medvee V. H., Madey S. F., and Gilovich T. "When less is more; counterfactual thinking and satisfaction among Olympic medalists." *Journal of Personality and Social Psychology,* 69, no. 4 (1995): 603–10.

CHAPTER THREE

Initially, most smokers: Centers for Disease Control and Prevention. "Smoking-Attributable Mortality, Years of Potential Life Lost, and Productivity Losses—United States 2000–2004." *Morbidity and Mortality Weekly Report;* http://www.cdc.gov/mmwr/preview/mmwrhtml/mm5745a3.htm; Behan D. F., Eriksen M. P., Lin Y. "Economic Effects of Environmental Tobacco Smoke Report." Schaumburg, IL: Society of Actuaries; 2005.

CHAPTER FOUR

Our beliefs and thoughts: Carpenter, Jeff. "Women Can Smell Genetic Differences." ABC News, Jan. 22, abcnews.go.com/Health/Depression/story?id=117027; Harvard Medical School. "Putting the placebo effect to work." Harvard Health Letter, April 2012; www.health.harvard.edu/newsletters/Harvard_Health_Letter/2012/April/putting-the-placebo-effect-to-work

CHAPTER FIVE

In 2009, pop star Kesha: Seventeen Magazine. "Ke$ha: More Outspoken Than Ever." *Seventeen Magazine,* seventeen.com/entertainment/features/kesha-pictures-quotes; Telling, Gillian. "Ke$ha's Mom: Weight Bullying Could Have Killed My Daughter." *People Magazine,* Jan. 20, 2014. http://www.people.com/people/article/0,,20777153,00.html.

BTP Tip: Show me the money: http://rady.ucsd.edu/docs/faculty/Fryer

CHAPTER NINE

The most extreme reaction to extreme thinking is the rapidly increasing rate of suicides in this country: DeNinno, Nadine. "Madison Holleran Suicide: UPenn Freshman Jumps

To Death Over Grades At Ivy League College." *International Business Times*, Jan 21, 2014. ibtimes.com/madison-holleran-suicide-upenn-freshman-jumps-death-over-grades-ivy-league-college-1544739.

CHAPTER TEN

In one experiment: Oswalk, Andrew J. and Daniel J. Zizzo. "Are People Willing to Pay to Reduce Others' Incomes?" *Annales d'Economie et de Statistique*, ENSAE, issue 63-64, pages 39-65. http://ideas.repec.org/p/wrk/warwec/568.html

This reaction of comparing yourself to others is not reserved for humans: Brosnan, S. F., & De Waal, F. B. M. (2003). "Monkeys reject unequal pay." *Nature*, no. 425, 297?299.

Research shows: http://www.health.harvard.edu/newsletters/Harvard_Mental_Health_Letter/2011/November/in-praise-of-gratitude

BTP Tip: Employees didn't receive appreciation: Ibid.

Loneliness: Cacioppo, John T. *Loneliness: Human Nature and the Need for Social Connection*. New York: W. W. Norton & Company (August 17, 2008).

CHAPTER ELEVEN

Patty Stonesifer: Hannon, Kerry. "Ex-Microsoft Exec Living The Boomer Fantasy: Meaningful Work." *Forbes*, June 24, 2013; forbes.com/sites/kerryhannon/2013/06/05/ex-microsoft-exec-living-the-boomer-fantasy-meaningful-work/2; Hendrix, Steve. "Patty Stonesifer, former CEO of Gates Foundation, to lead D.C. food pantry." *The Washington Post*, Jan 29, 2013; washingtonpost.com/local/patty-stonesifer-former-ceo-of-gates-foundation-to-lead-dc-food-pantry/2013/01/29/18da5ab2-698f-11e2-ada3-d86a4806d5ee_story.html

Increases your happiness: authentichappiness.sas.upenn.edu/newsletter.aspx?id=74

CHAPTER TWELVE

Oscar winner Lupita Nyong'o spoke: "Lupita Nyong'o Delivers Moving 'Black Women in Hollywood' Acceptance Speech." Essence Magazine, Feb 28, 2014; http://www.essence.com/2014/02/27/lupita-nyongo-delivers-moving-black-women-hollywood-acceptance-speech/

About the Author

D R. ELIZABETH LOMBARDO began her professional career as a physical therapist after getting her Master's degree at Duke University. It was then that she realized that every goal we have—whether it is related to our bodies, relationships, work or life—requires a significant mental edge in order to achieve it.

In her quest to help her clients actualize their dreams, Elizabeth went back to school to get her Ph.D. in clinical psychology. Wanting to help people "before they need a couch," Elizabeth now coaches, consults, and speaks to groups about how to achieve their desired results. Her first book, *A Happy You: Your Ultimate Prescription for Happiness,* is a national bestseller.

Elizabeth is a highly sought-after speaker and media consultant. She is frequently interviewed by today's top media outlets, including *Forbes, Wall Street Journal, Money Magazine, Health*, MSNBC, *USA Today*, CNN, and National Public Radio. She has made multiple appearances on *The Today Show.*

She lives in Chicago with her family.

Selected Titles from Seal Press

The 3-Day Reset: Restore Your Cravings For Healthy Foods in Three Easy, Empowering Days, by Pooja Mottl. $22.00, 978-1-58005-527-7. These 10 simple resets target and revamp your eating habits in practical, three-day increments.

Pretty Neat: The Buttoned-Up Way to Get Organized and Let Go of Perfection, by Alicia Rockmore and Sarah Welch. $14.95, 978-1-58005-309-9. Funny, irreverent, entertaining, and helpful, *Pretty Neat* offers readers unorthodox, surprisingly simple methods to reduce clutter-induced stress, and insists that perfection is impossible—and unnecessary—in this messy, unpredictable world called real life.

Yogalosophy: 28 Days to the Ultimate Mind-Body Makeover, by Mandy Ingber. $18.00, 978-1-58005-445-4. Celebrity yoga instructor Mandy Ingber offers a realistic, flexible, daily plan that will help readers transform their minds, their bodies, and their lives.

Undecided: How to Ditch the Endless Quest for Perfect and Find the Career—and Life—That's Right for You, by Barbara Kelley and Shannon Kelley. $16.95, 978-1-58005-341-9. Mother and daughter Barbara and Shannon Kelley explore how women's choices have evolved, why it's so overwhelming, and what we can do about it—starting with a serious shift in perspective.

Maxed Out: American Moms on the Brink, by Katrina Alcorn. $16.00, 978-1-58005-523-9. Weaving in surprising research about the dysfunction between the careers and home lives of working mothers, as well as the consequences to women's health, Katrina Alcorn tells a deeply personal story about "having it all," failing miserably, and what comes after.

A Cluttered Life: Searching for God, Serenity, and My Missing Keys, by Pesi Dinnerstein. $17.00, 978-1-58005-310-5. A chronicle of Pesi Dinnerstein's touching, quirky, and often comic search for order and simplicity amid an onslaught of relentless interruptions.

Find Seal Press Online
www.SealPress.com
www.Facebook.com/SealPress
Twitter: @SealPress